HONEY CHICKEN

Honey Chicken

My tragic and humorous
spiral into perinatal OCD

a memoir

By
Nola Lee Samuels

This is a work of memoir. The events described are based on the author's experiences and recollections. Some names and identifying details may have been changed to protect privacy.

Published by Nola Lee Samuels
Petaluma, California

Paperback 9798234109224
Hardcover 9798234148094
Ebook 9798234109248

Book design (cover & typesetting) by Barış Sehri
please visit *sehricoverdesign.com* for more
Typeset in Ashbury 10,5/15pt

First edition

For Matias & Romi – I'd go through it
all a million times for you two.

And for Jonah – thank you for never
giving up on us. I love you.

"The boundary line between the girl and
the woman is crossed in silence."
– Mary Cholmondeley, *Red Pottage*

"I could be bounded in a nutshell and count myself a king
of infinite space, were it not that I have bad dreams."
– William Shakespeare, *Hamlet* (Act 2, Scene 2)

Contents

Author's Note

This book contains sensitive subject matter. There was a time when reading even just a chapter of this book would have triggered me and sent me into a spiral. For this reason, I would like to warn the reader that this is not an easy book to read, especially for those that struggle with OCD, anorexia-nervosa, and/or postpartum depression. I have tried to cope with my mental health struggles by using self-deprecating humor, but these conditions are nothing to joke about. The purpose of this book is to destigmatize the internal shame that new mothers feel, as well as to start a conversation about a topic that has too long been ignored: maternal mental health.

Introduction

I didn't think I'd write this book. First, because I didn't think I'd ever get back to a place where I recognized myself again. Second, because describing exactly *how* a mental illness feels is incredibly difficult. I was apprehensive that I wouldn't be able to put it into words, and if I ended up writing the book, I would just confuse the reader and misrepresent the community I now belong to.

The real reason I decided to write the book was to try to heal. I wanted to undergo a catharsis so profound that it would shake the core of who I was. The meat of the writing was done in real time, whenever I was lucid or awake enough to journal about how I felt. I daydreamed, toying with the idea of one day writing a memoir or novel, of creating something tangible that I could hold in my hands, proof that I had overcome something huge. I also wanted to be able to pass the experience down to my children when they were adults, giving them a look into my life the way my parents had given me a look into theirs through photographs.

When I was finally diagnosed with the disorder, I scoured the internet for resources. I found research papers chock-full of medical jargon, but I couldn't find any memoirs that focused on the same situation I found myself in. I pored through message forums on mommy websites, and although there were obviously a lot of moms with anxiety, reading one paragraph about someone else's mental breakdown didn't make me feel any less alone. There were no explanations for why I was experiencing intrusive thoughts or nightmares so vivid that I would wake up in a sweat every night. No one was breaking down why I absolutely had to make sure my underwear didn't touch the ground, or any other surface, before I put it on. When I couldn't find what I was looking for, I decided to compile my writing in a book of essays, which eventually turned into this novel-like memoir.

I realize this book is sad, but it is also joyful. I didn't want the reader to finish and feel sorry for the shitty few years I've had. Just the opposite – I want the reader to feel empowered by my experiences. I want to shed light on the fact that pregnancy isn't pretty. It's raw, difficult, beautiful and brutal, all at once. I hope expecting parents read this book. I hope the partners of birthing parents, especially those whose partners may be dealing with OCD, come away with a better understanding of what that experience can feel like while bringing a child into the world.

Although this book may be difficult to read in places, I don't want the reader to miss the joy throughout. The joy of becoming a mother, the joy of finding someone in life to fight tooth and nail for, the joy of finding oneself again. Even though I was diagnosed with a mental illness, I know I hit the jackpot. I have two beautiful children and a loving husband. I am very lucky.

There are also people who will read this book and maybe recognize themselves between the lines. I see you, and I love you.

I want to clarify that I know how complex and messy families are. I know how complex and messy I am. Everyone has a side of the story, and everyone has a right to their own memory. Interpersonal relationships are difficult, and part of the human experience is being able to discern when something is done intentionally or unintentionally. Sometimes, we have the best of intentions, and we still fuck up. If I have misrepresented something involving you, I'm sorry.

I am moving forward. I am learning how to be present for myself, my family, and my loved ones. I am learning to temper my temper, to realize that I will never be able to achieve perfection. I am thankful for those who have stuck by me on this road. I love you, I see you, and I want to thank you for your support. It hasn't been easy, but my, oh my, it's been beautiful.

Chapter One: **Glass House**

There are glass shards all over the linoleum floor. I am wringing my hands, biting my upper lip, tasting the tang of blood. I hear children outside playing flag football, and I can't move at all. Matias babbles and coos ten feet away in the living room, safe in his bassinet. This is the first day on my own, the first day without my mom here, the first day I've been left to my own devices with my baby, our dog, and our new home. We have just moved to Sitka, Alaska, land of bears, Russian churches, and isolation. There is nothing here but vast beauty and a surplus of ravens. They land on the roof of our military townhouse and stomp around like they are performing a tap number. I think of Gwen Verdon in some Fosse number.

I weave my way through the glass shards on my tiptoes. *Stupid, stupid, stupid fucking idiot.* I want to scream because I've just fucked up everything. Everything is now contaminated and ruined in this new house, just because I dropped a mason jar from the freezer. I rewind the steps in my head, pissing myself off even more for letting my mom put glass jars of bolognese sauce in the freezer. *Stupid, stupid.* My heart is pounding and my hands are clammy and shaky as I realize I'll never be able to know for certain whether all the tiny pieces and particles of glass are gone. I could pick up a sliver on my sock and bring it into bed, and then when Matias lies on the bed, he could get it in his mouth, and it could cut up his esophagus and the stomach lining, and he could slowly die. Or Blu could get some on her mouth and bring it to the couch, where when I sit and put my hand down, it could get on my hand, and then I could rub my eye and blind myself. Or I could clean up the glass, and then, if I don't shower, some could get on my shirt, and when I lift my shirt to change, some could get in my bra and then in Matias's mouth when he nurses and ultimately hurt him. I can't even type the *k*-word. It'll set me off into the land of magical thinking, where I can control the survival or demise of any individual based solely on my telekinetic abilities.

I'm fucking crazy.

And it would all be my fault.

I slowly get the broom and sweep up the large pieces, trying not to picture the news story about the woman who unknowingly killed her family with glass microparticles on the kitchen floor. I pinch my hand to try to reset my brain. Like always, it never works.

§

One time last year, before my brain turned to mush, I tried to get rid of a broken water glass in the garbage disposal. I thought it was a pretty good idea at the time, plus I was too lazy to pick it out. Jonah ran into the kitchen when he heard the noise of the poor disposal, working hard to choke down glass shards.

"What are you doing, Nola?!" he exclaimed, looking at me with exasperation and confusion. I was so carefree then. I didn't even think anything of it.

§

Dangerous and stupid, I mutter under my breath, and my baby watches me with wide eyes from across the room. The pieces stick to the dustpan and I shake them into the trash can, feeling like I've sealed my son's fate. *Everyone is going to call me a bad mother, and I don't deserve to have a baby. I'm a fucking asshole.*

I start crying a little as I try to clean up, throwing the broom and dustpan off the porch into the grass below. Trash, trash, trash. Unclean and ruined. The kitchen is still contaminated and there are still little pieces of sparkly glass on the floor. There's no way I'll be able to get them all. This breaks me into a sweat.

I take the mini vacuum and try that. Then I use a wet paper towel to pat the floor for tiny pieces, but there might be tiny particles that got under the stove and fridge and into the far corners. Worse, there might be some on my socks, or maybe the wind pushed them onto my face and chest when I dumped the dustpan outside. My postpartum muffin top peeks out of my leggings, and I'm leaking breast milk onto my shirt, soaking it through. I haven't changed my shirt in at least twelve hours, and it smells like sour milk.

Gross. I think I'm so gross.

With every step I take to clean the kitchen, I make it worse. I call my mother and plead with her.

"Take him outside, Nola. Just go on a walk."

I strap Matias into the carrier, of course realizing moments later that there might be shards on my chest. *Oh no, oh no, oh no.* I'm certain I've made it worse. Matias looks up at his mama with big eyes, no clue what's happening.

Va tutto bene amore mio, Mamma ci sistemerà tutto. Tranquillo.

He blinks twice, and I fake a smile. *I am NOT okay.*

§

In the shower, I listen for Matias in his crib, gnawing on his elephant toy. My body is lobster red from scrubbing, my hands scaly, bloody, and humiliating. I hide them in public so people don't think I'm unfit to be a mother. They bleed constantly, so every sheet we own has random spots of my blood on it. Now there's blood in the bottom of the bathtub, and I dissociate, watching it fade into the drain, spiraling down into the abyss.

Leaning up against the cold tile, I put my head in my hands and squeeze the sides of my head ever so slightly. I rack my brain, trying to think of what I possibly could have touched between washing my hands and touching my face now – and what it might do to me. I do this for what seems like the millionth time today. Everything is just so dirty.

I use shampoo twice, closing my eyes and dreaming of a time when I wasn't bullied by my own brain. I read a book in college about a girl with a "brain on fire," and I understand more than ever now what she meant. At the time, I almost read the book like a study, so bewildered by how the brain could literally drive someone to insanity and into an asylum. Now I get it.

Matias is crying and I try to clean the possible particles of glass from my boobs, my skin, my hair, and my mind. They won't go away, and I sit on the edge of the tub, tears mixing with the burning water hitting my face. I need to get out and dry off and tend to my baby, who's making little noises now, wondering when his next meal is coming, probably. He's so innocent and doesn't know anything yet except the warmth of my arms and the taste of my milk.

He deserves a mother who's able to pick up broken glass on the floor, someone who doesn't cry at the drop of a hat over some minor inconvenience. A mother who can walk through an airport with confidence or help him try new foods and make new friends. Not a mother he'll have to reluctantly explain to his friends one day.

Yeah, MY mom, she's crazy.

Dried off, I pick up my sweet baby, and he nestles into my chest, his tiny hands gripping my clean shirt and wet hair. I want to kiss his cheek, but I think I have a canker sore, and maybe I might give him something – which, of course, I don't have, but WebMD convinced me I might. For all I know, I could've picked up herpes at the dentist's office last week.

I'm so utterly exhausted, and I can't even relax in the moments when I am supposed to be soaking in the newborn bliss. Whether it's fear of getting avian flu from the raven poop outside, or spider venom on the newly clean clothes, or lead poisoning from the balsamic vinegar with the Prop 65 warning, I'm in my own personal hell.

Drowning in worry. Never has that phrase held more meaning for me.

I don't exist apart from my anxiety; it has taken over every facet of my life, controlling the minutiae of my everyday life, stealing headspace that's supposed to be filled with JOY. It makes me absolutely furious when people say that it doesn't seem like I'm enjoying having a baby.

That's not true. Matias is the best thing that has ever happened to me. What I'm not enjoying is the anxiety, panic, and fear.

Meds are looming in the near future, and I even have the prescription for Zoloft. I put it in the hall closet, on top of the board games and sheet music. I have to call the doctor back to update her on my progress. The truth is, I haven't even taken one pill, and I don't plan on doing it, even if I get to the point where I'd have to go to a clinic.

Because, because – what if the medication makes me go blind? Or kills me?

I don't want to take medication. I don't want to worry about my breastmilk being laced with drugs, or that I won't wake up in the night when Matias cries. I'm worried it won't work and I'll just end up addicted, savoring each pill like I did when I was a Xanax enthusiast.

Just take it, for God's sake.

Well, what do they say about nursing while taking meds?

You know, you can't just cover it up with a metaphorical Band-Aid.

I've heard all of these opinions, and it makes the decision

to take them or not even more excruciating. Damned if I do, damned if I don't.

But I know deep down I won't take them. *Fuck no.*

In those rare moments when I do want to try them, I can imagine a world where I am relaxed, where the little things don't bother me anymore. I envision myself as this cool mom, able to let my kid run outside barefoot in the mud like I did when I was growing up. Now I'm worried about the poisonous mushrooms outside our front door and whether or not the spores have spread all over the yard. Jonah spent an afternoon pouring four gallons of white vinegar on them, probably freaking our neighbors out. I watched him from the window, surveying his progress and worried it wasn't enough.

It's even scary imagining Matias crawling around the floor of our house. But maybe if I try the medicine, it'll be okay. Something inside me is telling me not to take it, but trusting my own intuition is not something I've ever been great at. My track record is absolute shit. I fell for every man I shouldn't have, tried every drug I was offered, and never spoke up for myself. I let myself get walked over like a dog, deifying those experiences as part of my "life journey." I should've wanted to emulate someone like Ruth Bader Ginsburg instead of Amy Winehouse.

§

Jonah comes home from the unit, and I fall into his arms, ready for him to relieve some of the stress I've been carrying on my back all day. He holds Matias and plays with him. I stir my cup of lactation tea and curl my feet up under my knees on the folding chair at the dining room table, worn out after my mental marathon. Jonah flips through the channels, and Matias sleeps in his arms, snoring softly.

I text my therapist and give him a rundown of the day, rubbing my eyes with the back of my clean hand, careful not to press on the tear ducts too hard. I can't believe I have to wake up tomorrow and do this shit again. More worry, piling on. Sisyphus had it easier. At least he had just one thing to worry about, even if that worry never ended. I feel more like Atlas, holding up my entire world.

§

I pray to God each night, the same prayer, with my hand on Matias the same way every time.

Dear God, please make sure our baby boy Matias is safe and healthy. Thank you, God, Amen. Baruch atah adonai eloheinu melech ha'olam.

I cup my son's head in my palm, and he smiles in his sleep, eyelids fluttering as he dreams. I love him more than anything in the world. The Alaskan sun isn't even down yet, and a warm glow seeps through the blinds, hitting my back as I continue to lean over and stare at him.

He's perfect. He sucks his little thumb while asleep, lying on his left side, legs pushing up against the side of the crib near the bed where I sleep. He'll end up in bed, snuggled in next to me as he nurses and his dad snores at the other edge of the bed, arms askew and legs hanging over the edge.

§

I wake up throughout the night in a panic, bad dreams dragging me awake to the thought that the worst has occurred. SIDS rolls around my brain like a ball in a pinball machine. Even writing the acronym seems like a bad omen, a premonition. I can barely even write it.

I sit in the yellow chair I was nursed in as a baby, and I scroll through dozens of articles about SIDS, trying to figure out if anything Matias has been exposed to could contribute to risk. He's three and a half months old. At one year, he's almost safe. That is, if I can avoid tobacco, pollutants, and all forever chemicals until then. Easy.

Nine months is such a long time, and I want to have at least one more child. I know I can go through anything again. I'm tough. But realistically, I don't know how much more my marriage can take. If OCD shadows us for the entirety of another pregnancy, it'll put a crack in the foundation, eventually taking us down.

I listen for the shallow breathing coming from the crib. *Okay, he's breathing. Calma. Calma.*

I miss being a kid, a teenager, a young adult, when my worst fear was not making it on Broadway, or having them fuck up my order at Chipotle. Jonah shifts in his sleep and throws his legs over the covers. I hold my breath and listen to the symphony of inhalations and exhalations coming from my husband and son. It almost sounds like a song I've heard before.

What time signature is that? It's rhythmic, and I listen until sleep finds me too. The Northern Lights dance through the sky above us on our little Pacific island, peaceful and wild.

Chapter Two: **Bathtubs**

We're huddled in the cracked bathtub in our Tulsa rental. Minutes before, sirens sounded throughout the neighborhood, letting us know a tornado was supposedly ripping through the city. Jonah shakes me awake and yells for me to go to the bathroom quickly. He throws the mattress over his back and follows me, motioning for me to sit in the tub while he covers us as much as he can with the gigantic mattress, sheets hanging off.

Our dogs, Blu and Yak, get in the bathroom with us as Jonah shuts the door. Blu whimpers and tries to crawl into the tub with us, while Yak, the miniature husky, is completely unaware. He pants and looks at us with a blank stare, sitting by the door with his ears perked. Jonah sits with his back to the leaky faucet, which drips ominously as we prepare for the worst. The wind slams against the windows of the house, creating intense pressure. All I can think about is *The Wizard of Oz* as I touch my belly. Blu is hanging over the side, shaking and squealing, and I watch my new husband grit his teeth and suck air in through his mouth, trying to appear brave.

I know he's scared shitless.

§

That morning we confirmed that I was pregnant. This was June 16, and six days earlier, we had gotten married. On the last day of our honeymoon, Florida was hit by an epic tropical storm, and while Jonah flipped through TV channels to check the evacuation orders, I snuck away to the bathroom to take a pregnancy test. I had been bizarre the past few days and, even before our wedding, had opted out of using the hot tub for unknown reasons.

I just don't feel like it, I told my men of honor.

Palm trees were bending as the rain drove into the ground. I peed on the stick and waited while I listened to Fox News in the background. I wanted a baby badly, and I doubted that it could have happened this fast. One time of not being careful – that would be almost impressive. I crossed my fingers and crossed myself, a move close to sacrilegious, seeing as I am not Catholic.

The two pink lines appeared and I almost choked. *It happened.* I was going to be a mother.

I had imagined this moment so many times in my life: the arrival of the two little pink lines, and the unmistakable pregnancy glow. There had been so many false alarms, tests taken in the Rome Fiumicino Airport, the bathrooms at Penn Station, and even in an airplane. The difference now was that I wasn't panicking; I was hopeful.

I looked in the mirror and touched my lower belly. There was a baby in there. Our baby.

Rain was pounding down on the windows of my in-laws'

condo, where were staying, and I ran out to Jonah.

"I'm pregnant!" I said, in a voice at least an octave higher than the one I usually use.

Jonah looked over at me, smiling nervously as he checked the weather and evacuation notices. He was in a state of panic. We were sitting multiple floors up, in a condo complex a stone's throw from the ocean. If there was a weather emergency, we would be the first ones to know.

"That's great, but I need to figure out if we need to book it out of here or not."

He smiled in a way that told me that he couldn't multitask at the moment – that this was definitely not the optimal time to find out I was pregnant. I am extremely talented when it comes to choosing the worst time to say or do anything. It's always at the last minute, or when something major is happening, that I decide to drop whatever information bomb I've been holding in.

My face fell, and I marched back into the bathroom. No Instagram-worthy reaction for me. I know most of those amazing husband reactions online are rehearsed, but *Hey, let's make sure we're not going to die in a tropical storm*, felt a little underwhelming at best. I stood in the bathroom, staring at my tummy again in the mirror. Jonah came in and gave me a hug, and we packed up.

"I'm really happy, Nola," he said. "I just want to make sure we can get out of here safely before I have a proper reaction."

Fair. He was compartmentalizing his feelings, like he is prone to do. Jonah puts one feeling in one mental box, another in another, and keeps them separated.

We drove back to Oklahoma as expectant parents through the wind, rain, and flooding. It was a nightmare on those highways, with two dogs in the car and a baby in my belly. The storm was horrific, and at one point we pulled over at a gas station in a flood zone, Jonah going into the store to buy provisions as I sat and prayed to every deity I could possibly name.

All I wanted to do was get home to Oklahoma to dust and dry heat, where we could test again and celebrate in relief. Until then, everything felt dicey, from the slippery highways to the cars slicing through the rain way too close to our Subaru. I ate soggy fries in the front seat, texting nervously as I pored through articles on my phone during the drive, learning I needed to start eating significantly more for the baby that was growing.

§

And here we were now, cramped limbs in the bathtub as we waited for disaster. My sister-in-law, a native Okie, let us know that we were officially fucked if we heard the unmistakable sound of a train whistle. We wait for that sound as the house shudders and wind rolls over the poorly constructed roof. Glass breaks in our bedroom, and a tree falls in the backyard, hitting our roof.

Fuck. I look at Jonah, and I can tell he's gritting his teeth, white-knuckling the mattress above us.

What if we don't make it? What if this baby in my belly never gets to experience grass on their feet or wind in their hair or, or, or the ocean? What if these are the last few moments of our lives, and we're sitting in a disgusting bathtub?

Jonah's pants and shirt are soaking wet by this point. The leaky faucet is loud even though the wind sounds like people screaming outside, hitting our windows with gusto and pushing in harder. Branches crack, and I hear something hit our roof.

Please God. Broken glass, somewhere.

"Hold on," Jonah says, looking at me. "Why the fuck did we move to Oklahoma?"

We both laugh, in hysterics. I have to pee. He's been holding our mattress for over an hour and a half, and the wind is still roaring. I keep rubbing my belly. He notices and grimaces.

It's a sick joke. We can't catch a fucking break.

§

We slept that night in the living room, the safest room, out of the way of possible falling trees. The dogs curled up around us, weathering the storm by insulating us with thick fur. The moonlight bounced off the wood floors, and we lay nose to nose. *I love you,* we said with our eyes, and we fell asleep, hoping we'd wake up.

I dream of Dorothy and Toto. One of the dogs poops in the corner.

§

Tulsa is a ghost town the next morning. Our bedroom window is cracked, and a huge tree branch has landed on top of the roof, barely missing where we sleep. I kick through the debris in our backyard, stunned. Not even Dunkin' Donuts is open, and there is no power. We drive in silence, barely recognizing our neighborhood. Hundred-year-old trees are ripped out of the ground, creating massive divots in yards that look like sinkholes. Telephone lines are sagging and down. The tornado touched down here but barely missed our house.

Power will be out, and everyone's on their porches, sweating in the Okie heat. No refrigerator, no fans, no light. Slow livin' with packs of Coke and pork rinds, red dirt country playin' on the radio. Folks walk between their neighbors' houses, surveying the damage. I see two men trying to lift a tree off a van, arms straining, faces flushed beneath grimy baseball caps.

Oklahoma gives me a bit of a reality check. This is how the rest of the country lives. It's a flyover state, and no one comes here to visit. The history is rich and dark and it feels haunted. We're living on Native land, and it feels like stealing. Tulsa's remains of Black Wall Street are in plain view, yet the rest of the country seems to have forgotten about the Tulsa Massacre. I admittedly hadn't even heard about it before I subbed a class at the school where I teach.

We go to Target, where looters have already taken advantage of the situation. People are wandering through the aisles like zombies, some browsing and trying to check out and be good people, others running back through the sliding doors with frozen waffles and electronics under both arms. I am tempted, but I married a saint. Maybe not a saint, but someone obsessed with morality and ethics.

We don't take anything, of course not. Jonah wants to buy

food for all the homeless people on the corner, even though we have, like, zero dollars. We go to the freezer section and stand in front of the glass. The condensation on the doors is almost pretty, and the ice cream and frozen goods are starting to melt from the lack of electricity. We opt for mint chocolate ice cream for breakfast, heading through the store as it's being looted. My ice cream is slush before we get to the cash register.

§

Three days before, we were browsing a bookstore in Destin, Florida, looking for books on pregnancy. I was already starting to feel on edge, nervous about everything I was eating. *Is it too spicy? Does it contain additives or sulfates?* Jonah tried to get us to go to the Italian coffee shop we had frequented every morning. I would have none of it. I wanted coffee badly, but now I knew that everything I put in my body was either going to positively or negatively affect our baby.

"Jonah, coffee is DANGEROUS for the baby!"

He'd mutter under his breath and suggest something else. I picked out a book at the store for "naturally inclined" pregnant women and read the entire thing at the kitchen table over a day and a half. Jonah tried to get me to go to the beach, but I told him there were more important things to do now. It didn't even hit me that we were on our honeymoon and I was sitting there at the table – studying, of all things.

The book was terrifying and graphic. There was so much that was scary in there... so many things that could go wrong...

so many dangers. Stuff I hadn't even imagined could be dangerous, suddenly was. My hands were now clammy just thinking of tropical diseases.

This is normal, I thought. *Everyone must go through this.*

§

In bed at night, I lay awake, trying not to touch my stomach, lest I damage the baby by accidentally resting my hands on it too heavily. I went through the roster of diseases I knew existed and landed on measles as the most likely for me to catch.

Not for one moment did I pause to reflect on how ironic it was that I was worried about anything when our baby had already gone through a tropical storm and a tornado and was apparently thriving. I had absolutely no clue that another storm was coming that would actually sweep me off my feet.

This storm, however, was invisible to everyone but me.

Chapter Three: **Everything Is Terrifying**

Growing up, I wasn't really afraid of anything. The exceptions to this were the typical fears of death, quicksand, and making my parents mad.

My parents have been married for over thirty years. We always knew their marriage and love were steadfast and would never dissipate, and I didn't doubt it for one minute. It's obvious even today that my parents are still madly in love. When they got engaged on the side of the road in Copperopolis, California, my mama made my papa promise to buy chickens, get his goddamn skis off the wall, and never divorce her. He said that sounded all right, and they got hitched. This was followed by a crazy whim to sell all their crap and travel the world for a year, after which they bummed it in a van while trying to find a place to settle down for ten months before deciding on Colorado.

They have a love for the ages. In fact, I probably had unrealistic expectations when I was hoping to find a partner. I wanted someone like my dad, who is just the most mild-mannered man of all time. He goes along with everything. This made it really easy for my mom to wear the pants – which was healthy and unhealthy for me and my sister to see. On one hand, she was a strong woman; on the other, she could be obstinate and stubborn.

If I had to put my finger on it, the aspects of my dad I set out to find in a man were simplicity and honesty. My dad has liked his stuff, his way, since the beginning of time. This means he's been wearing the same 501 Levi's since adolescence, and he keeps his non-organic Costco food in the extra fridge out in the garage, away from the bushels of kale and stinky kombucha that line the kitchen refrigerator's shelves.

§

During their travels, my parents lost their sense of caution. I think my mom was always an adrenaline junkie, and that, combined with my papa's insane athleticism and desire to climb and jump off things, made for a set of parents who scared the shit out of us.

"Don't let fear control your life!" my mom would scream as we tubed down Boulder Creek with lightning cracking above. Shivering, I prayed to the God they didn't believe in, promising I'd practice violin without complaint if we'd only get through this alive.

My parents were under the impression that life wasn't worth living if you didn't take risks, and they pushed us to believe the same. My dad would always mention the "cost-benefit analysis" of any given decision, inviting us to wager the good of a choice versus the bad, and exactly how much risk the decision would create. My mom always told me everything makes a good story one day, and that we are the sum of our experiences – good or bad. We were exposed to and taught concepts that were light years beyond our comprehension, because, in my mother's eyes, that was true education. She sat me down in front of the TV to watch the horrifying film *Kids* with her when I was thirteen. I was scarred for life, and finished the movie hiding behind my hands, convinced I was going to contract AIDS if I did so much as touch a boy. My mom believed that by sheltering us, she wouldn't be protecting us. "Knowledge is power" was her mantra.

§

We went on river-rafting trips every summer as kids in Southern Utah. I didn't love these trips, as the outdoorsy bug never actually bit me. I already knew I belonged in a city. I was so inept at rafting that I'd often fall out of the big, blue raft, learning early how to safely let the current take me to more tranquil water. Sometimes, though, the waves would be rough, and below the surface there would be logs and sticks, reaching up to grab my feet and hold fast. Laughing nervously to hide her fear, my mom would wait for me on the riverbank while I swept downriver.

The Morrisseys aren't pussies! Where's that strong Irish resolve?! She thought this was encouraging.

I glared at her in my ill-fitting swimsuit, triangles askew, wanting to kick something. She raised her eyebrows, bristling, warning me not to cop an attitude. I knew that getting upset would turn into an afternoon of fighting about how the life education we were receiving was something any kid would kill for.

§

Whenever my mom felt that residual Catholic guilt, she would treat us, giving us a little trinket from her box of treasures, or perhaps a meal of hand-pulled noodles at our favorite restaurant.

The problem was, at the drop of a hat, she would take the gift back, telling us we didn't deserve it any longer. One week, I remember memorizing a concerto on violin, and she surprised me with a pair of Japanese flip-flops with tatami material on the footbed. I was elated. They were cool as hell. But the next day, when I didn't practice two hours straight on my instrument, she took them away. I think I threw a tantrum, not my first and not my last.

My mum was all about instructional justice and tough love. An upstate New Yorker by birth, she never lost that intensity and grit people love and hate about New York, even though she left as a little girl. It's a harshness and brutal honesty that serves a person well in court on the stand, but not many other places. On top of that, she lived for years as a child in Tanzania. Thrown into the wilderness, I'm certain she experienced things I couldn't even dream of. She and her brother learned Swahili and spent their days running around their Dar es Salaam neighborhood with labradors and chickens while my grandparents worked in medicine.

§

I love looking at photos of my mom as a kid, because I can't draw on any experience from my own life. Her childhood was so wildly different from mine. Snooping around her closet, I would put my face close to her old 4x6 photos, trying to see if I could perhaps smell Africa. I did smell cigarettes, but not much else. I lay with my belly down on our Middle Eastern rugs in the sun, nag champa incense burning somewhere in the house, Norah Jones playing in the background on our modern stereo system. I rifled through her things, looking at pictures I wasn't supposed to see and trying on Maasai jewelry I wasn't supposed to touch. She had and still has so many beautiful things, and it was a treasure trove. Hours would pass as I dug through my parents' underwear drawers, reading snippets of their travel journals, after which I felt my first pangs of guilt.

I was so sneaky as a kid and would lie randomly if I thought the story was better. I wanted to know who my parents were before me, because that's when it seemed to me life was good for them. My dad's first days in Kathmandu or his climbing expeditions, my mum's months spent in Jamaica working at the Kingston Library – it was better than the books I was given to read, and those were almost equally exciting. *The Brothers Karamazov*, *A Tree Grows in Brooklyn*, *I Know Why The Caged Bird Sings* – I lived to read. I devoured literature, sitting in the thrifted chairs in our living room, picking at my toenails and petting our overweight pugs. When my mom would run errands, I took advantage of the time alone and went into all the deepest corners of the house. It was, and still is, a poorly organized museum, beautiful paintings and artifacts collecting dust among carabiners and old climbing ropes.

I am still under the impression that my parents can't die. They seem immortal, almost, and I can't imagine a world without them, where I don't call them on the phone daily to shoot the shit. They are the best storytellers, weaving sagas with their words as they show us slides from their youth. My dad, getting attacked by a monkey while they backpacked through India, both skinny, having puked their guts out after bad food. They spoke of the worst of times as some of the best because it fed the flame of their adventure.

My mom hopped on a plane to Nepal at eighteen, driven by her dad having led the first expedition up the East Face of Everest. She took photographs that should be in *National Geographic*. Her talent really is unmatched, and yet her work won't ever be seen by the masses. My photographer husband thinks she's the best photographer he knows. She pushes aside compliments and changes the subject when it comes up.

It doesn't matter, I can hear her say, *I didn't DO anything with it.*

I'm sure my mom will live forever, but every time my dad goes up to his property in the mountains to drink beer and throw frisbees on his disc golf course, I say a little prayer that he'll come back. I've had so many dreams of finding out he's disappeared up there. As horrific as this sounds, I think it suits him. I wouldn't be surprised if twenty years from now, he just vanishes in those dry mountains one night while wandering on his property, never to be seen again among the sage brush and fossils. He has a love for the land that is marvelous. I don't appreciate nature that much, but I was raised by a man who lives and breathes granite and pine.

§

This generation is obsessed with the "beige aesthetic" and the phenomenon of the "sad, beige mom." It's quite sad because, to me, a big part of the wonder of childhood is the color and brightness and excitement of being young and free of responsibility. What kid wants to grow up wearing only sand, onyx, slate, or camel? It's depressing, really. My son's room already looks like Elton John and Liberace's dreamscape. I grew up in full color, from the red of my skinned knees to the green of the foliage we ran through daily at our Boulder home. Why would we try to manipulate the aesthetic of someone so young?

Let kids be kids.

§

We were allowed to run wild, but there was intense discipline too. I had to practice violin every day, and that was a constant in my life from age six until eighteen. I loved the violin but hated practicing. It was the worst, and I would fight my mom on the length of the practice damn near every day. By the time we were done fighting, an hour would have already passed, and I'd have to keep going until my hour was up. Sometimes it was two.

§

I loved *Fiddler on the Roof* more than anything. I kept begging to play the fiddle, and then when I met my longtime friend Jens at kindergarten and saw him play, I pleaded with my mother to let me start. She conceded, and she ended up falling in love with it more than I did. She got me started with one of the best teachers of the local Suzuki program, and I was initiated into hell. My teacher had me come to lessons every Monday morning at 6 a.m. Imagine getting a child up the first day of the week to be chided and shamed by a music teacher. Pure torture. The worst part was that I had to have everything prepared that she assigned me the week before, and if I wasn't ready, I was guilted or threatened, told she might drop me as a student if I wasn't serious. *Please drop me,* I'd think, but instead I'd just work harder and get more and more mad inside. Who the fuck threatens a ten-year-old, saying if they don't memorize an entire movement of a Haydn concerto in a week, they'll be dropped and perhaps music isn't for them? I call bullshit. I mean, even Gypsy Rose would think that was too much.

My week was full of music. Monday mornings at 6 a.m., I had a private lesson before school, then Tuesdays I had Irish fiddle lessons, Wednesdays I had orchestra, where I got teased mercilessly, but at least my dad took me out for a burrito afterward, and then Fridays were the hell of all hells: GROUP VIOLIN. This was two hours of music theory and group practice, where you were actually singled out if you weren't prepared. Jens and I would leave school early like everyone else on a Friday, eat our lunch, and be driven to the church for Group. We begged the heavens for a disastrous miracle or a bomb to save us from the weekly inferno we were about to endure. We begged our parents to let us skip. When this didn't work, we'd fake a fever.

None of it ever worked. They'd drop us off, and we'd trudge into the Methodist Church in South Boulder, grumbling. I was so afraid that I hadn't prepared enough and that I would be humiliated. I almost always pulled through, but it was still a nightmare having to perform every week, especially next to the little Chinese girl who was flying past me in her ability. My mom would push her elbow into me at our spring concerts while we watched her play, homemade poofy dress, hair in the tightest ponytail known to man, her mom sitting in the front row, tight-lipped with her video camera. The OG Kris Kardashian. *Wow,* my mom would always say, ***aren't you glad I'm not like that?*** I'd unintentionally gawk at her.

My fears, though, were based on potential consequences. I was so worried that I was going to anger, or worse, disappoint my mom. Violin was just the perfect scapegoat I could put all those fears into. All the feelings I ever had, all the anxiety – I siphoned it into the act of practicing my violin. All the anger I had at my mom came out when I was forced to play. When she would hum along, I'd purposely fuck up the notes so she stopped singing. It felt like fingernails on a chalkboard to me.

Uh oh, she'd say, *that's definitely not the right note.*

I'd glare over the fingerboard of my instrument, jutting my hip out in defiance.

You don't know that, I would say, then close my eyes so I could have some privacy.

She had this way about her that made me feel I couldn't trust myself to make any decisions alone, because I knew she knew better. Or knew what was better for me. I still hesitate and start sweating when I have to make a decision, even one as simple as what brand of hummus to buy, or what color shirt would look better on me. Some people talk about hearing God's voice in their head; well, mine was my mother's. It is just as ominous and unsettling as the God voice you hear in old movies, but it scares me much more. This fear conditioned me to be blindly led by her taste and her opinion, so much so that I let others who I ended up loving or respecting make choices for me as an adult. I said, "Jesus take the wheel," during so many crucial moments of my life, I am surprised I am alive. I never worried about death, or disease, or germs. I was only afraid of what my mom would think. And to be honest? I probably still am.

Chapter Four: **Windows to the Soul**

When I was born, my mom knew something wasn't quite right. She was ecstatic about my birth, and she and my dad were extremely happy, but she remembers bringing me home and noticing that something wasn't right with my left eye. There were, it seemed, spiderwebs crossing the surface of my retina.

She brought me to the pediatric eye doctor, and five days later, the newborn me was stretched out on an operating table, given general anesthesia, and operated on. My mother wouldn't let me go when they took me to the operating room – she was apparently wailing and begging them to take her eye and give it to me. Tiger Mom was born at that moment.

I can picture her, with her strong stature, making a scene, scared her baby wouldn't be coming back. It broke my heart, but I didn't realize the full extent of that kind of heartbreak until I became a mother. Nor did I understand my mother and how she did her best, loving us, albeit too much sometimes, but all the same, loving us.

What I was diagnosed with was called PHPV – persistent hyperplastic primary vitreous disorder. It is incredibly rare and is difficult to explain, so using the *Finding Nemo* analogy usually works. Like Nemo, I was born with a birth defect, a bum eye instead of a bum fin. My eye didn't fully develop in utero – we don't know why – and it stopped growing. The eyeball itself became more akin to a football than a basketball. This meant that they had to cauterize a pupil during surgery, leaving me with white marks around my pupil, surrounded by a blue rim. On the best of days, it looks like heterochromia.

The eye is technically blind, but my parents were determined to give me a fighting chance by working the eye to the point of developing some vision. They wanted me to get my backup eye in as good a shape as possible, just in case, God forbid, something happened to my healthy eye. This is the reason I spent my screen time as a child literally glued to the TV. They patched my good eye, forcing me, for the first seven years of my life, to watch television with limited vision, exercising the eye that was legally blind.

It worked. I gained the ability to distinguish shapes, light, and movement. The doctors were so impressed with my parents' resolve and commitment, and with me. I was tiny at the time, so I hadn't yet experienced bullying. My parents knew that was coming, but they were still living in the space of making sure I was healthy. Every day as a newborn, my mom would place a speculum in my eye. She held my head and body between her legs, trying not to cry, scared I would end up hating her because of this necessary torture she had to put me through every day.

The condition is not hereditary; it's a complete and utter fluke. I grew up knowing that my kids wouldn't have to go through this, but when I thought of pregnancy, I was always a tiny bit frightened that maybe, just maybe, the doctors were wrong and I would pass it down to my daughter or son.

I loved my eye as a little girl. I thought I was special because I had one brown eye and one blue eye. My sister would draw me as an angel, my eyes bigger than saucers on the paper, a halo above me, wings on my shoulders, and the colors so pronounced in the drawing that my eyes popped on the page.

§

That changed with school. I went from being special to different. That wasn't as good. People didn't know what to do with me because my eyes were not normal. I combed my wild hair back and went to class each day with a huge smile, spirit still not broken, ready to take on the world with gumption. I wore cargo shorts and my mom's costume jewelry, accompanied by an ugly pair of Keens. But I loved how I looked.

You're weird. Your eye is freaky.

I remember hearing that for the first time in second grade. I'm sure I did hear it beforehand, but I can remember this moment so clearly because it was the first time I can recall feeling ugly. The other little girls had matching eyes, and when we learned about symmetry and geometry, the teacher told us people are drawn to this – symmetry meant beauty.

To compensate for feeling insecure, I became a social butterfly, but not a cool one. I was a total dork, talking and laughing too much in class, while also reading everything I could get my hands on. It took me until third grade to read, but once I did,

I took off – much to the surprise of the teacher who thought I was mentally handicapped because of my eyes. She was truly an idiot.

My parents never let me feel sorry for myself, though. Every time I asked them why I came out of Mommy's belly with these eyes, they would tell me it was because there is beauty in individuality and uniqueness. They made me try all the sports, including swim team, where I got many teal participation ribbons over the course of a few years. I wasn't a good swimmer, but that wasn't what made me stop. One of the boys, swimming in the lane next to me, started harassing me about my eyes, saying things so mean I have all but blocked most of them out.

When my mom figured out what was happening, she swooped in so fast that the kid quit the swim team. I don't know what she said to him, but she scared him shitless.

§

In middle and high school, I began feeling like no one would ever like me – at least, no one *I* liked. The boys thought I was pretty, except for my eyes. I remember hearing my crush say this to one of my friends outside at recess. He didn't know I could hear him. I think that was the day my self-confidence died. It destroyed me. I sat behind the swings in my baggy jeans and hand-me-down Juicy Couture sweatshirt and cried. I never wanted to go back to class again. I never wanted to talk to my crush again. It wasn't like I wore glasses he didn't like – he was repelled by something that, no matter how hard I tried, I'd never be able to change.

§

In tenth grade, I hit my limit. I begged my parents to let me get surgery and replace my eye. I wanted to fit in; I couldn't do this anymore. I was willing to try anything at that point.

The Indian American eye surgeon was smart as a whip. He was new on the scene and used to seeing young kids come in for surgeries. In the waiting room, my mom struck up a conversation with another mom from Texas. Her high schooler, quiet and frowning, sat next to her, with bandages all over his face.

His uncle beat cancer, she said, quietly, as if he wasn't there, *so he set off fireworks at a party for him. Something backfired, and they blew up into his face. He still has gunpowder lodged in his face, though, so we can't operate.* She crossed her legs and looked over at her son. He was still silent.

The doctor told me I had a few options. He said I could do a total evisceration, where they would take out my eye completely and replace it with one made of some sort of coral, where afterward my optic nerve would grow around the eye, giving it the ability to track somewhat well. I squirmed in my seat, pins and needles all over my legs. I was really upset by the idea of taking out my eye completely. The doctor, in his opinion, thought it would be best to go with the second option, where I would undergo a surgery to pull the Gunderson flap – a flap of tissue at the bottom of one's eyelid – up over the eye, sewing it closed to desensitize it. This would make it possible for me to have a scleral shell. The doctor also was adamant about saving my bad eye, just in case something happened to my good eye later in life.

You need a backup, he said. *Accidents happen.*

My dad looked like he was about to cry in the corner of the room. He was standing with his arms in the pockets of his Patagonia fleece, eyes scrunched up, so tiny I could barely see them. I felt really weird, especially when the doctor mentioned the fact that my eye was just atrophying slowly and would eventually die. I wanted to vomit in the little trash can next to the door.

§

A month later, I went in for surgery. My mom, my dad, and my cousin Peter accompanied me to the eye clinic in Denver. I was silent the entire ride down to the city, Peter holding my hand, my mom and dad giving me pep talks to prepare me. My mom kept saying that it wasn't a crazy surgery and would be over quickly.

The IV didn't take several times, and already bruised and uncomfortable, I was finally put under. The last thing I remember is being wheeled into the operating room, and a doctor in a mask with glasses lifting up my gown and putting weird suction things on my chest. It was most likely to monitor my vitals, but I remember being upset before I passed out, not liking to be touched.

According to my family, when I woke up, I was incoherent, speaking about having fought in the Civil War. Peter took me to the bathroom, where I began singing, loudly, still drugged out, high as a kite. I almost fell off the toilet, and it took us half an hour to get me to go pee and leave the restroom. He practically carried me back to the recovery bed.

On the way home, I demanded a burrito. I was starving, and when they wheeled me out in the wheelchair into the sunlight outside, that was the only thing I wanted. The whole way home, I had my eyes closed, listening to my family speaking quietly about nothing. We stopped at the mall, and my dad ran in to get me food. I scarfed it all in the car, and immediately upon returning home, vomited in the guest bathroom by the garage. Not my best moment – the doctor had told me not to eat following surgery.

§

A day after my surgery, I realized I wasn't able to see much at all with my good eye. For some reason, it was having a sympathetic response to the trauma in my bad eye and wasn't cooperating. Peter and my mom changed my bandages, and I lay in bed like the Union soldier I had dreamed of being, letting them feed me soup and eggs and saltines. Every time I tried to use my good eye, it was as if someone was shining a flashlight directly in it, or like I was staring directly into the sun. I gave up and just kept my eyes closed – using them just gave me a terrible headache.

§

I spent two weeks in the bed downstairs, where my mom set up a cassette tape of Homer's *Odyssey* for me. When a side on the tape would end, she would come downstairs with more eye drops and flip it over. I loved Greek classics, but I was getting bored and scared. I wondered if my vision would ever return. No one was talking about it in front of me, and that seemed like a bad sign. At my check up, the doctor was quick and quiet, checking everything while barely saying anything. I started to freak out but remained stoic in front of everyone else.

I kept thinking about what I would do if I went blind, if my eyes never worked again. I was grateful to have my other senses, because they all became heightened in those weeks. I leaned into listening, smelling, and feeling everything. I could tell the time of day by the smells coming from upstairs – coffee in the early morning before my dad left for work, and pollen, soil, and budding flowers midday when my mom came in from gardening. I could smell the dirt under her nails when she adjusted the pillow under my head and hear the clinking of her thick gold ring against the plate as she fed me toast with peach jam.

It turned out my eye didn't like being sewn closed, and the stitches split a few weeks after the initial surgery. The doctor marveled at how strong my eye was, complimenting me. I didn't want compliments; I wanted the surgery to work. Because of this, they operated again.

§

Tenth grade was halfway through, and when I went back to school, I had to wear an eyepatch. I went for the black patch, trying to copy the villain nurse from *Pulp Fiction*. She was sexy and could pull it off. I, on the other hand, had no boobs to speak of and no access to a sultry nurse outfit. No one got the reference anyway. Instead, I started counting the number of times each day someone would mention pirates when I walked past. My friend Jens even started calling me "The Angel of Death" when we performed eurythmy in white robes for the Christmas festival at our Waldorf school. I moved across the stage with all the grace I could muster, confidence shot but determined not to bow out. I still look at pictures and cringe. Oh, to be young.

§

On my walk to the bus after school through the neighborhood in North Boulder, the same homeless guy would taunt me every day, good-natured maybe, but infuriating nonetheless.

Where's your parrot? Got any cash, er, buried treasure to share? Every day he said this, and every day he would laugh himself into a tizzy, finishing with a coughing fit.

I really wanted to tell him to go get a job, but I was scared of how he'd react. My mom told me it was building character, and to let it go. I started taking a longer route to school.

§

We were studying Chaucer that semester, and I couldn't get into it. I was still in some pain, and I was in my first actual relationship. Halfway through the school day, I would lie down on the couch in the schoolhouse living room, resting my eyes while my new boyfriend rubbed my back. That was the upside. I think the only reason that period was relatively easy was because I had someone who said he was falling in love with me. I want to applaud my high school boyfriend. He was solid, never making me feel less than for patching an eye, and never making it a big deal. We're still friends.

§

I secretly started to obsess about losing vision in my good eye. Anxiety would creep in at night, and I would go into the bathroom and rinse my eye with hot water in the shower, scared there were tiny bits of glass or dust in there. Looking back now, I see all the warning signs of obsessive-compulsive disorder, from the boiling water to the need to make sure my pillowcase was new every night, so I wouldn't get a soft-tissue infection and blind myself. I started to spend way too much time thinking about blindness.

§

I was fitted for my first scleral shell six months after surgery, in an office that smelled like what I imagined chemotherapy would smell like – noxious gas and stale air. The Artist took an imprint of my eye, showing me the ridges and grooves, the irregularities of my eye post-surgery. I couldn't see the blue tie-dye color anymore, and my bad eye was now worse, covered up by flesh. It freaked me out to look. I could see the thread of the stitches and the red of the scar tissue, and it looked monstrous.

He matched my eye color and the white of my eyes, taking hours at a time to send us to the nearest food court while he worked on the eye. My mom and I sipped on Diet Cokes and walked through Abercrombie & Fitch while we waited, me squinting my eyes while we perused, not wanting anyone to get a peek at my now hideous eye. My mom bought me jeans and a few shirts, even a jar of the signature perfume. She wanted to make it special, and that signature smell still makes me smile and think of my mom. It also smells like a New York nightclub that I used to go to in my twenties.

When the scleral shell was finished, the Artist made minor adjustments before feeling good enough to show me his work. I suddenly felt embarrassed, not wanting my parents to be there. I felt like their reactions would be good no matter how accurate or inaccurate the shell was in mimicking my good eye. He took a suction cup and, prying my eye open with his big sausage fingers, inserted the shell, now attached by suction to the little tool. He adjusted the shell within my eye, showing me how to place it so that it wouldn't move around. It wasn't comfortable in the slightest. What's that old adage? *Beauty is pain.*

I turned around in the chair and looked at myself in the mirror. I wasn't expecting much; I didn't want to end up disappointed. What I saw made me stand up straighter. I now had two brown eyes. Not identical, not perfect, but passable as normal. No one would do a double take unless they were making deep eye contact with me – I could move through the day without worrying about what someone in the car next to us would think when we stopped at a light.

Standing up, I stepped back. I was gangly, my body awkward, in the middle of puberty, and my hair pushed back behind my ears. I looked closely at the artistry, moving my eyes side to side to see how much tracking power I had. There was a good amount, just not when I looked all the way to the left. I made a mental note not to look that way anymore and looked at the Artist.

Thank you, I said. *I love it. I think it really works.*

He gruffly nodded and shook my parents' hands. My mom was sobbing silently.

Chapter Five: **Anorexia, or, the Death of My Personality**

Day one of pregnancy, and my anorexia completely and inexplicably disappeared. I guess I found the only thing worth eating for, and for that I am grateful. That is the one positive that came out of mental anguish – I swapped one mental illness for another. I started to gain weight fast, drinking a gallon of vat-pasteurized milk every couple of days, intent on loading up on carbs like a marathon runner, even though the only marathon I was competing in was one with myself on Netflix. I didn't think once about whether I was going to lose my glorious thigh gap, it just was. That was what had to happen for me to birth a healthy baby. My jeans, even just a month into the first trimester, wouldn't fit. I shrugged off my chunk and threw on a pair of Jonah's sweats. *The fuck if I care,* I thought to myself every day. *The fuck if I care.*

Anorexia hid my mild OCD for many years. I was able to push through those mental and physical compulsions by literally cutting my brain off at the source. When I starved myself, I took conscience, reason, and logic out of the mix and replaced them with a blank and vapid personality. It all makes sense now. I can see little glimpses of obsessive behavior during periods of my life that were swallowed up by me starving myself.

So why did I go down the road of starving myself? A myriad of reasons.

Contrary to popular belief, most of the time people don't starve themselves because they want to be thin. There is always an underlying reason for losing and then keeping off all that weight. Whether it's a persistent need to control, or a desire to forget or dissociate, eating disorders always boil down to one thing – the desire to make oneself invisible.

§

When Jonah and I first got together, I was ninety-eight pounds. My arms were like sticks, and he would hold them in his hands.

You're like a baby bird, he'd say.

My whole family calls me Nola Bird, I told him. *It was also my first word.*

He shook his head and leaned against the counter of the Lake House in East Texas.

Uh... he walked around the island, rubbing his five o'clock shadow, obviously uncomfortable. *I really don't want to be with someone who is slowly killing themself.*

My mouth dropped open. I was offended, and it felt like an ultimatum. At the time, I was surviving on Diet Coke, cigarettes, corn tortillas, and flour mixed with raw egg and sprinkles. Disgusting. I thought he was crazy. I was HOT. I had long, skinny legs and a miraculous gap between my thighs. I could see my collarbones and ribs and cheekbones. I barely made a dent when

I sat on the couch. I was proud of myself, and I was an artist. I didn't need food to sustain me. I was like Carrie Bradshaw, and I'd rather read *Vogue* than eat food. Like she famously quipped, "It fills me up more." I tapped my acrylic nails on the counter and looked him in the eyes, challenging him. He crossed his arms, and we stopped talking about it.

At that point, he didn't know the real reason I wouldn't eat. I probably was so brain-dead from exhaustion and undereating that I hadn't figured it out myself. But now that we're here, and I'm older and wiser, I've figured it out.

§

There are three reasons I chose to subsist on barely 700 calories a day for years:

After all the eye surgeries and issues with my vision, I wanted to feel in control and feel beautiful. I felt like my face would never be symmetrical or pretty, so I vowed to make my body covetable and damn near perfect.

Two, men liked women who looked like models. Ipso facto, I wanted to look modelesque and garner attention for my looks. I never felt like guys had liked me, and I wanted revenge. I was in the business of breaking hearts, or at least I thought I was. The reality was, I was good at picking up losers and then trying to fix them until I realized they were unfixable.

And three, I was molested as a child by someone very close to me. This last reason was the driving factor behind everything in my life. I drank, I starved myself, I took pills. I searched for validation anywhere I could find it, because my childhood had felt like a betrayal. The memories came flooding back to me on my twenty-fourth birthday while I was living in New York. It ruined the day, as well as any semblance of normalcy and stability I had at the time. The memories were triggered by an ex-boyfriend popping open a can of Diet Pepsi. It was as simple as that.

I had a good childhood, apart from this. I thought I'd emerged unscathed from my early years, a menagerie of decent core memories with me, moments in time I would cherish forever. That still is the case, but a lot of memories have been tainted now that I finally understand what was going on. The abuse explained my constant need to please people, no matter how much it put me out or hurt me. I wasn't bothered by inconvenience; I cared more about what other people thought and wanted than what I wanted or needed. I needed so badly to be liked and wanted.

I realized why I didn't like to be tickled, why I didn't feel comfortable with people touching my chest or the small of my back. Those things always gave me an icky feeling and would make me shut down. Now all that behavior had an explanation, and I was angry.

§

In the wave of the #MeToo movement, I was drowning in flashbacks and in the pain of people close to me doubting me, or believing me and not taking any steps to help. It felt almost ironic that at one of the most pivotal moments in women's rights in the United States, people who were posting that they were supportive of victims were, in fact, protecting a perpetrator.

I guess everything is different when you are actually in a situation where someone you know has been hurt, but my logic was, *Wouldn't that make you MORE angry?* I kept thinking of the idea that an innocent bystander who does nothing is also guilty in their own way. I wanted to scream to get people to hear me, and I started to shut down and not eat, feeling like I was maybe not worthy of love, or that it didn't matter that I was sexually abused.

I still have nightmares where I am getting married and my abuser shows up, demanding to know why I didn't invite him, belligerent about not being able to know my sons. I stammer something and shut down, and he tries to hug me again.

I saw him once a year after the memories resurfaced and had a visceral reaction to his smile and touch. He tried to hug me and shimmy his hand up under my boob, and I quickly stepped back.

I guess I'm not allowed to kiss you, right? For a second, I thought someone had told him. No one had. I'm sure he knows, though.

Haha, what? My hands were so clammy.

He laughed, and I awkwardly went to the fridge to get an orange La Croix. I stood around the party for a few minutes, starting to hear the crescendo of the pounding in my head. I knew this was a panic attack and pushed my way through people chatting and getting day-drunk on rosé and chardonnay to beeline for the bathroom. I sat on the toilet, legs involuntarily bouncing off the seat, teeth chattering, shaking uncontrollably. I could barely walk back out the screen door to the brunch party. I went into one of the bedrooms and put on a gigantic hoodie.

Through the next few painful hours, I sweated through my many layers of clothes. I kept the hoodie on even when we went to the beach. Everyone was in sundresses and linen, and I looked like I was at an audition for *The Outsiders*. I didn't want him to be able to make out any curves or lines of my body. I was done being a Lolita, a role I never knew I had played close to my entire life.

§

It still makes me sick to think about. The surf broke as I wandered down the beach, away from the people. I watched my toes disappear into gray sand, my hair and face already salty from the spray off the Pacific. I continued into the ocean up to my knees, already drenched but not feeling anything, completely numb. *What if I kept walking?*

The starvation bit was a way for me to disconnect and leave my body. If I wasn't eating, I wasn't thinking, and then I was happier, even though I was making riskier decisions that put my body and my mind in danger. Unprotected sex, pills and weed, too much alcohol – all these felt like great ways to escape my mind and thoughts. The thing about these unhealthy Band-Aids is, when you stop them, all you're left with is *you*.

When I stopped drinking, I had to start coming to terms with the fact that I was pretty stunted emotionally. I had this obsessive need to please and make everyone love me. I never wanted to be alone, and I used online shopping and weird diets as a way to distract myself from the fact that I didn't like myself very much. I spent money I didn't have on manicures and clothing, going into debt and not saying a word to anyone even when I knew I was drowning in unpaid bills. When I stopped all this and wasn't able to constantly distract myself, I had to get to know myself again. I really didn't know who I was without those quick fixes.

The funny thing about anorexia is that it's a game. The goal is to lose so much weight that you *win*, while cooking and baking up a storm and encouraging those around you to indulge more. Everyone I know who has struggled with an eating disorder has had a compulsive need to bring their friends and family and even colleagues baked goods. It felt so good to watch other people get fatter. That sounds terrible, but it's true. Spending hours on Pinterest looking at vegan food was a way to eat with my eyes, while I lay there in bed, starving after my dinner of a summer peach and four Brazil nuts.

§

My therapist in Los Angeles dropped me because I kept skirting around going to a recovery clinic. I legitimately thought I was fine, and she said I needed to go, and I said no, and she flat out told me that she couldn't help me.

I can't help you. No one can help you. Help yourself.

I sat in her chic office, complete with a $7,000 rug and designer chairs, and smiled while thinking, *Fuck you.* She was this beautiful woman – Botox, facelift, boob job, makeup, and skinny as a twig. *Help yourself, my ass.* I ran away and straight into a liquor store for a bottle of Bombay Sapphire. I was delusional, but convinced myself that was all the calories I needed for the day. Gin is food too.

Sample Food Diary from years 2013 to 2022:

4 a.m. half a Bobo bar

6:30 a.m. coffee with a tablespoon of coconut milk

9 a.m. coconut flour mixed with cacao nibs, water, and flaxseed flakes

10 a.m. green tea, two tea bags

3 p.m. salad with half a bottle of Braggs nutritional yeast

6:30 p.m. a bag of baby carrots

8 p.m. mezcal and lime La Croix

I was truly starving myself. I would walk with my knees held high, like a baby dinosaur, unsure of my footing. I lost so much hair that my tub drain clogged every month, and I had a light layer of peach fuzz everywhere, the kind your body produces when you're severely malnourished. My fingernails were bumpy and uneven, and I had zits that would pop up on my chin every week. Standing in front of a full-length mirror I could count my ribs, and when I'd wear a shirt, my sternum and collarbone would poke out. I have countless selfies in changing rooms at Target and Nordstrom where, at the time, I'd stare at my body in disgust, convinced my thighs were huge and my arms unsightly. My proportions were off, they were off, they were off. I'd journal and conceive of a plan to lose more weight, adding five packets of Splenda or stevia to my coffee instead of a little honey, or opting out of purchasing sweet potatoes that week. It was in those moments that I made the most dangerous decisions regarding my physical health. I kept pushing a little further, a little further. No one knew the lengths I went to in order to have that thigh gap.

The selfies, in retrospect, are something out of a horror movie. I looked like a prisoner of war. Most of all, my eyes look vacant. My personality had left the building. Looking back, I guess my OCD contributed to my need to stay a certain weight. I was ever so meticulous about my food intake, counting my baby carrots, making sure everything was eaten or cut up into even numbers. The problem was – well, one of the problems – was that I couldn't recognize the obsessive behavior because drug, alcohol, and anorexia dependency were in the way. The light was so obscured by these four things that I felt like I was wading through swamplands, every morning willing myself to get out of bed so that I could get to it – ensuring a "successful" day by numbing myself the fuck out until I couldn't feel those bad feelings anymore.

Anorexia steals your individuality. I would read a book and then realize I didn't remember anything. I failed my college exams one semester because I realized I couldn't retain any information subsisting solely on Diet Coke and white bread. My college routine was yoga twice a day, two cans of tuna, one latte, five hours of ballet, two Diet Cokes, and as many oranges and slices of white bread as I could steal from the kitchen at the convent. The whole thought process around white bread for weight loss is still an issue, and I can blame Signora Cinzia for that.

§

My host mother, Cinzia, in Sardinia, invited me to try the "prison diet" with her, as she'd seen that I'd put on a few pounds and used to sit in the field by the house eating peanut butter out of the jar my mom sent from the States.

Prison diet? I asked.

Si, she said, *it is a surefire way to lose weight. Prisoners are skinny, and all they eat is bread and water. I promise we will lose weight and look good.* I paused.

Like prisoners? I asked.

Yes, good. Like prisoners. She looked over the balcony at the street below and threw down her cigarette.

The Prison Diet is as miserable as it sounds. We were both bloated from too much water and processed white carbs. In Italy, some of the white bread is made with lard, which makes it absolutely delicious but also extremely bad for your cardiovascular system. Between the overconsumption of lard, the bottled water, and Cinzia's pack a day, we weren't really the picture of health. We were in one of the world's Blue Zones, eating like shit and probably shortening our lifespans by a considerable number of years, when ironically, everyone else was living to be over a hundred, eating veggies and pasta and wine, and feeling way better than the two of us. Ridiculous.

I bowed out and tried the liquid diet. I had seen my mom try going for a week drinking a concoction of water, lemon, and maple syrup. It was one of those early diet fads of the 2000s, where every soccer mom was trying to lose weight fast by legitimately starving herself. Such a good idea, this was. I made it through the first day, and by the next morning, I was weak, shaking, with super low blood sugar. I actually crawled down the stairs at my host family's house and into the kitchen. I made five peanut butter and jelly sandwiches and sat on the concrete steps in the back, scarfing down sustenance while the pigeons ran on the laundry line. I vowed to never actually starve myself again. Starving in Italy is almost an oxymoron.

§

Today, food is just a way for me to fill up my boobs with milk. I eat at lightning speed, in the rare moments when my baby is sleeping, playing with his toys, or blissfully in his Dada's arms. Between the effort it actually takes to make good food and the money it takes to eat out, I alternate between fried eggs on toast and one of the many cheap pastas I have mastered. I can barely even sit down for a cup of coffee in the morning now without the dog pooping on the carpet of the baby's room or the washer breaking because I accidentally threw the remote in before the wash cycle. Food and anorexia are the last thing on my mind, and honestly, I'm glad. My body has given me so much – I am a mother, and I grew a child inside my womb for nine months, then completed the miraculous feat of birthing him into the world. I feed him through breastfeeding, and he is growing big and strong because of the nutrients I give him through my milk. I'm a goddamn Wonder Woman; every mother is.

I think I can get past the need to be ninety-eight pounds. That is, if I ever manage to step into a restaurant again without thinking I'm going to contract listeria.

Chapter Six: **Matias Is Born**

One Monday morning, six months into my pregnancy, I diagnosed myself with perinatal OCD. It only took four hours of typing, *Why am I so crazy while pregnant?* into Google to source reasons that I had, in fact, gone off the rails completely. This turned into researching – obsessively, of course – different mental disorders that could affect women during this time. I was sitting – always sedentary – quarantined in my childhood bedroom while Jonah was at boot camp. Slumped over at the old wooden desk, hand sanitizer next to me, eating tahini toast with two fingers, trying to keep anything that went into my mouth clean, clean, clean, I scrolled down through the endless list. I stopped at OCD. I read the blurb, highlighting the symptoms of obsessive-compulsive disorder.

Oh, shit. Everything I was reading was hitting a nerve. I recognized myself in the laundry list of symptoms.

The dog barked outside, and I heard the murmur of my various family members downstairs, making coffee, doing finances, avoiding me. I had been living with my parents in Colorado for a few months, which was hellish, at best.

I kept reading. The article explained that women with perinatal OCD obsess over fears, which turn into mental rumination or physical impulses that continue the cycle of obsession. Ultimately, it said, OCD gets worse and worse the more you lean into the compulsions. It is usually accompanied by disturbing intrusive thoughts and doubt, fear, and disgust with oneself. Guilt is a huge component as well. *Welp.* That was me. Reading on, I discovered that perinatal OCD affects just a tiny percent of the population.

Just my fucking luck. I swallowed loudly and looked down at my growing belly, moving as the baby kicked my ribs. The one thing I wanted was to be a mom, and it's the one thing that would trigger a mental disorder that makes me feel like my brain is broken. It's almost ironic.

Why, God, why? What's the point in handing me this challenge? Wasn't having a bum left eye enough? Or being molested as a child? I was already working on overcoming hardship. Why'd you have to hand me another one? Ugh. This blows.

I waddled downstairs in my pajama pants and oversized T-shirt and alerted my parents that I thought I had OCD.

We know, they said, *and you're holding us all captive.*

I had been waging war with them, my grandmother, Jonah, and anyone else who dared defy what kept my unborn child safe. I guilted my mom enough that she removed all plants from the house. There were over fifteen plants sitting in pots everywhere, from the kitchen counter to the foyer. It felt like I was avoiding landmines of toxoplasmosis. When she went to see a friend who had a cat, I would spiral, making sure she removed her clothes when coming into the house and then washed them in boiling water to remove any chance of contaminating the house with cat dander.

What the fuck is wrong with you? I yelled at her. *Why don't you want to keep your grandson safe?*

She would get angry back at me, and we would fight for hours on end, each of us becoming increasingly volatile and mean. My papa was like the sitting duck in the middle of it, neutral as Switzerland, but still mad at me, occasionally losing his shit. He told me over and over again that I couldn't hijack their lifestyle – that they were sacrificing so much to make me feel comfortable. The thing is, they weren't making me feel comfortable; they were making me feel immense guilt.

That's true, I said, *but can't you go out of your way to please help me? I didn't sign up for this. I was expecting pregnancy and a baby, not a fucking mental fucking illness!*

Sick joke or not, I have to consciously not victimize myself. I tend to slide into martyrdom when I get bored or insecure, and I knew for my baby's sake that I wouldn't be able to get away with that anymore. But feeling crazy, or worse, being seen as crazy, is absolutely horrible.

§

So now, a week into postpartum, I feel absolutely fucking crazy, just like everyone says I am. I'm frozen. My teeth are chattering, and my mind is running a million miles per minute, coming up with theories that terrify me. I'm buzzing, my heart is beating like I ran a marathon, and I'm now substituting old theories for new ones. I'm almost amazed at the velocity at which my brain is able to speed me through dozens of horrifying scenarios, each feeling more real and immediate than the last. I am practically drooling, like some unkempt slob, unable to shut my mouth – *I hate my brain, I hate my brain,* I keep saying, as if that would help. No one understands me, but I'm really just keeping my baby safe. That's all that matters; that's all that matters. Maybe if I say another prayer or knock on wood three times, I can counteract the contamination that happened. But then again, maybe thinking those bad thoughts about the worst of the worst happening actually wills it into existence. I don't fucking know; the world is a mystery. *Couldn't hurt to try.* Plus, if I'm right, we will be safe. I will keep him safe.

The internet says these are panic attacks, that in those moments death feels imminent, and unless you're also afflicted by this shitty mental disorder, you won't ever understand. Ugh. I can't even write or say that word for fear of the consequences. Death, I mean. It makes me squirm just typing it again. Now I need to knock on wood again.

Even the word *imminent* feels wrong in my mouth, like a piece of candy that's been sitting in the car too long, something that you find in the back seat and suck on reluctantly. What I've been experiencing – these weird moments where I feel like I can't breathe – is totally normal for someone with my condition. Which, in essence, is funny, because I've been experiencing them for practically my entire life, only now more intensely and much more often.

My friend the internet explains it as the feeling of living in "fight or flight" every damn day. And when it's not fight or flight, it's freeze, where I dissociate and zone out, staring at the onesie

I'm about to put Matias in, or the soup I'm cooking on the stove. It's constant and debilitating. I'm living inside this shit.

§

From the moment I wake up, I'm trying to skirt around disaster, so utterly convinced that every choice, no matter how small, affects my baby's well-being and life. I'm exhausted. The only thing that keeps me grounded at all is caffeine, so I cling to my cup every morning, willing myself to keep doing normal human things, telling myself that everything is going to be okay, even if I'm triggered. The entire house feels like there are landmines everywhere, and if I can just tiptoe or treat everything like a possible explosive, we'll be okay. For the time being, anyway.

Lord, help me. Labor was easier than this.

§

Matias was born at 5:50 p.m. on a cold February evening. I was induced in order to make sure Jonah could be there before starting his position in the Coast Guard up north in Alaska, and what was supposed to be a long labor was sped up by the pills they gave me to create artificial contractions. My water broke naturally the morning after I took the first two, and I began experiencing pain, dull at first but growing fast, until within an hour I was contracting every minute and bearing down. I was told that I wasn't even dilated and that it was the beginning of labor. I gritted my teeth and was silent. I couldn't complain. As women, we are pushed to be quiet and full of grace when feeling discomfort. I told myself I could do it. The only way was through. My mom and the nurse got me in the tub. I hadn't taken a bath in nine months, and the water felt too hot and too foreign. I grabbed the edge of the tub, in so much pain.

Honey, this is only the beginning. It's going to get so much worse, my mom said, rubbing my back and fixing my long, ratted hair into a messy bun. I glared at the water, mad at her for not believing how painful this all was. This did not feel like early labor.

I still didn't cry. Every time my body was rocked by a contraction, I let them know calmly and bore down. I was fully in the present, and OCD had left my side. It was clear what I needed to do – experience what was happening moment to moment.

§

Years ago, I had written a note to myself: *Fear is replaced by trust.* I had spent my entire pregnancy swimming in fear, worried sick that my baby wasn't going to be all right. I avoided everything that could possibly cause damage to him or my body. I wouldn't get near cats or people who owned them, wouldn't touch fruit, vegetables, or plants because of possible toxoplasmosis. Everyone had to wear a mask around me, and after being exposed to COVID twice, I decided not to venture out anymore unless it meant going to the doctor's office. I panicked and called the nurse hotline every week, talked to a rep at poison control for half an hour, and dove deep into Reddit, asking everyone's opinions on eyedrops, honey, and soft cheese. I couldn't take the possibility that any given food might make me sick, so I lived on a diet of pasta al pomodoro, beans, rice, and peanut butter.

Nothing was enjoyable anymore, not even showering. I developed a nightly ritual that alone took about an hour, but halfway through, I would mess up slightly and have to start again. I had to be extremely clean. I would wash my hands before touching a new towel, strip down, take down my hair, brush my teeth, wash my hands again, get in the shower, wash my hair, wash my hands, wash my face, wash my hands, wash my body, wash my hands, wash the shower knob, get out, dry my hair and body, wash my hands, go pee, wash my hands, run into the bedroom, lay my towel on the bed, and proceed to get changed. This would involve walking on my tiptoes over to my drawers, opening them with my pinky finger, taking my underwear, and standing in the corner of the room. Then I would have to get my feet into the underwear leg holes without touching the sides. If I missed, I'd have to discard them and grab another pair. I even put my back out and gave myself sciatica by doing this in my seventh month of pregnancy.

§

I spent the last two months before giving birth hobbling around the house, unable to get down the stairs alone or get up to go to the bathroom. My mom had to sleep in bed with me to turn me over and push me up to the point where I would inhale fast in pain, hold my breath, and make it to the toilet. This was at least ten times a night by the eighth month. It was even hard using the bathroom and thinking I wasn't dirty afterward. I used so much hand sanitizer and vinegar spray during those last few months, I could have put the local Rite Aid out of business. My behavior was insane in retrospect, but it all felt extremely necessary at the time. I thought my anxiety and dread would all go away after Matias was born, but it got worse. I felt like a prisoner in my own mind – I still do a lot of the time.

§

In the delivery room on February 23, I sat in the bed, rocking back and forth, absolutely mute, squeezing Jonah and my mom's hands, hard. I felt like my body was rupturing like a volcano from the inside out, and all I could think of was whether Matias was okay. Minutes felt like hours, and the nurse hadn't checked to see how dilated I was in hours. Three hours in and convinced I was still in the early stages of labor, I opted not to get an epidural. But by the time it had been three hours, I was absolutely exhausted and wanted some relief. My body was shaking involuntarily, and I was spent, cold, and sweaty. Feeling like I was giving up, I said quietly that I wanted the epidural, that I was too spent. The anesthesiologist came in wearing pointed snakeskin boots, and by this time, I was shaking so hard I had to hold onto the nurse, my mom, and Jonah for stability. I was frightened by the idea of a needle in my spine, not so much the pain. Pain was irrelevant at this point. As he administered the meds, I finally let go and cried, bawling into the shoulder of the nurse, smelling her sweet perfume. She let me soak her shoulder in tears. I was so tired, and I just wanted my baby.

The sun lowered in the sky; I was 9 centimeters. I had labored the entire time without meds. I remember feeling so proud of myself. *See? I'm tough. See? See?* I started smiling as the medicine began to work. They kept giving me more juice, and by the time I needed to push, I felt ready and the pain had subsided. Now all I felt was intense pressure. I pushed for three more hours, and Jonah and my mom stayed by my side. The nurse kept telling me I wasn't going hard enough, and I sheepishly admitted I had OCD and was scared of rupturing my cornea and not being able to see my baby. She stopped and looked me in the eyes, giving me a pep talk. The room smelled like lavender, and it was starry outside. I could see my baby's head crowning, and my doctor came in, turning off all lights except for a spotlight positioned above me. For a minute, I drifted off to New York, standing on that stage in my black leotard, dust illuminated by that spotlight. It was my time to step up. It was our moment, mine and my baby's.

The doctor noticed a spot on Matias's head, almost like a blood blister. At that point, I panicked. *Is something wrong? What did I do wrong? Is he going to be okay?* I knew at that moment I needed to get him out. I needed to bear down and be brave and do what so many women had done before me. I looked up at the spotlight, blocking out everyone else. My contractions paused, and I waited for the next one, the big wave. Only Matias mattered.

I talked to God. I told him/her/whoever I was going to push

one more time, giving all the strength I had in my worn out, tired body. I felt warmth spread across my face, and I looked into the light, knowing that He was protecting my baby, and me.

Matias was born, and I sprayed our doctor with blood and amniotic fluid. I saw a conehead and wrinkly little grape body, hands splayed out in surprise. The cord was wrapped around our baby, and he was brought up to my chest. He was purple, and I pulled him against me.

My baby, my baby, my baby.

I cried big, salty tears. The nurse grabbed him from me and started suctioning fluid from his mouth and nose. At that point, I realized he had not cried. He was so tiny, six pounds, and so quiet. She worked furiously, and I started asking if he was okay repeatedly. No one would answer. I continued, raising my voice louder. Jonah was alternating between the baby and the space down by the doctor. I learned after the fact that I had torn horizontally and was losing blood fast as the doctor used gauze to keep me from going into shock while simultaneously sewing me up.

I didn't care how I was doing. I was solely focused on Matias. I held my breath for what seemed like minutes, until the nurse put him on my chest and quickly pulled a little cap over his head. He was so, so small and so, so beautiful. My ego left me at that moment, and my heart grew exponentially. I looked down at the beautiful creature that had grown in my tummy for close to a year. His hair was curly and dark, his eyes dark blue. He had his Dada's mouth, full and smiley. He made tiny little bird sounds and started instinctively nursing, his hand holding onto my chest, his eyes closed. My heartbeat was home to him. I stared into his eyes for hours, marveling at the amount of love I felt. Nothing else mattered, or matters at all. Just this perfect, precious little human who carries both me and Jonah. I have never felt happiness like that. Even just the feeling I got in that moment was worth every moment of panic, every fear, every day spent in isolation. I would do it a thousand times over for him. My Matias. My entire world.

Chapter Seven: **Omnia Vincit Amor**

I thought pregnancy was the hard part. I didn't realize that my anxiety would simply shift and morph into something different postpartum, or that my marriage would dissolve and rip apart at the seams.

Jonah was at boot camp during the entirety of my second trimester, and then at A School for the third trimester. We were technically newlyweds, and we were separated within a few weeks. We had absolutely zero communication during the eight weeks of boot camp, apart from me writing him a letter every single day. I did this because I loved him, but I was also bored out of my goddamn mind and experiencing pregnancy alone while living for a month and a half with his dad and stepmom in Houston, after which I moved to Colorado to be with my family. Hindsight is 20/20, and both ideas were horrible. I wasn't in the headspace to be around anyone apart from a full-time therapist, and they didn't understand why I was having a nervous breakdown every day.

I binge-watched *Desperate Housewives* and tried to document every symptom that I had every moment of the day. I kept a journal where I'd write down, "You're not a bad person," over and over again while I sat on the king-size bed, drinking steamed milk from the bakery down the street. It was so hot, all the time. There was an AC unit and a fan in the room, pointed at me while I lay back on the bed, trying not to melt. The croissant I ate while lying in bed crumbled on top of the duvet, and I was so unbothered that I didn't clean it up. I just slept in crumbs for a few weeks in the Texas heat. My belly was growing, and I remember thinking I was so huge at that time, when in reality, my baby was the size of an apricot in my uterus, and I wasn't even needing to wear maternity pants yet. In spite of this, I walked around like a woman nine and a half months pregnant, complaining about my back and swollen cankles. I didn't have a doctor for that period in Houston, and so for my prenatal needs, I found some shady office with an ultrasound machine by the airport. It was definitely not a legitimate medical facility, but I just wanted to make sure my baby was okay, and I had no insurance coverage at that point. I think it was next to a Dollar Tree. Frightening.

When I went to the OB for the first time in Oklahoma, she immediately asked me if Jonah and I were related. My jaw hit the floor, and I started laughing. We had just been asked a similar question when we got married, except the clerk at the town hall had specified his question, asking if we were cousins. We had doubled over, laughing at the audacity of the clerk. I guess this was the South. When I first went back home with Jonah to visit his home state, I was preparing to go out to dinner and worrying about my outfit. He waved off my concern, telling me: "Nola, this is East Texas. If you have all your teeth, you're a ten here."

The doctor looked at me with a blank stare and continued.

"Do you use meth?" she asked, nonplussed. I opened my

eyes wide and asked her if that was something she really had to worry about mothers-to-be doing.

"This is Oklahoma," she said. There's a lot of meth use."

I raised my eyebrows. Jonah looked at me. He was scared stiff to be in there, to become a dad. He was fidgeting next to me, picking at the plastic on the armrest of the chair. I could see him physically shaking from the weight of the responsibility he now felt.

"Are you related?" she asked again, almost frustrated.

I laughed out loud and told her that was the second time in the last three weeks that we had been asked that question.

"Ew, no," I replied, and I wrinkled my nose.

§

Things are so different now.

I can't remember the last time Jonah and I shared a knowing glance. Matias is barely a month old, and we don't talk. He helps me out, goes through the motions of changing diapers, holding him while I sleep, folding his clothes, but then he's out the door to go run in the snowy spring weather, leaving me to cry by myself on my childhood bed, nursing our baby until he falls asleep again. We don't kiss, we don't hug, we don't touch each other. There is a chasm between us.

Our relationship started to go south when I left for Colorado and began the process of micromanaging him through fear. I called him in Virginia, worried about the measles outbreak, telling him he couldn't even go to a drive-through to get a chocolate shake. He seethed silently on the phone and started to resent me – my never-ending interrogation, my constant fears about miscarriage, my anxiety. He never stopped calling every day, but he stopped actually talking. It felt like a ghost on the phone, going through the motions of what a husband does, but the marriage itself felt like a house of cards, shaky and unstable. I was talking to a wall, and it felt like the one person who was supposed to be on my team had left the chat completely. Granted, I never actually asked him how he felt, and never even thought about asking whether he was scared to become a father.

When he graduated and returned to Colorado before the doctor induced me, he was cold, barely hugging me or talking to me. His lips were insanely dry, and he didn't look me in the eye. His answers were curt and polite, and he went straight upstairs to shower, first putting his bags in the garage, lest they contaminate the house with "airport diseases."

The rest of the day was awkward as I tried to talk to him about the baby, about pregnancy, about how I was feeling. He nodded along while eating his egg salad sandwich, eyes glazed over. That night we got in our first big fight. I don't even remember what it was about, but I think it had to do with the fact that he wasn't encouraging me or making me feel better about the next day's induction. He lay on the other side of the bed, and I cried. I wanted him to touch my belly – which he didn't do – and tell me I was beautiful, that I was strong, that what I was doing and sacrificing was admirable and amazing. I bawled, and he got upset and sat in the rocking chair that was in the corner, waiting for our baby. I think he sat there all night, scared.

I didn't even want to get induced, I wanted to go into labor naturally. However, Jonah wouldn't have been able to attend our son's birth if I didn't go into labor in the five days he had before reporting. I was scared to get induced, but I felt it was important to give him the opportunity to experience Matias's birth, and I wanted him there with me – I probably wouldn't have chosen to go that route if I knew how badly the aftermath of that would go. In his defense, he didn't know how much of an asshole he was being.

Every morning, I wake up to the sun rising on the Colorado mountains, and my tiny baby who is a miniature version of his father, mewing for food. I dress him, unsure of myself, in his little onesie with pretzels on it, covering his fingers with socks so he doesn't scratch his eyes. Jonah comes into the room from his turn sleeping, and silently motions for me to get up. I'm relieved of my duties, and can go make French toast. I yawn and make my way downstairs to my parents and grandmother, who are drinking coffee and eating leftover birthday cake from my twenty-ninth birthday party the night before. I don't hug them, like usual, and my papa makes room for me to make my matcha.

I go through the motions, wiping my eyes with the inside of my shirt, pouring in maple syrup, washing my hands, then adding coconut milk, then washing my hands after I close the refrigerator door. My mom comes over and tentatively touches my shoulder. I flinch. *What did she touch before touching me?* She notices and backs off, asking if Jonah wants to eat with me. I make some excuse about how he's not hungry, but everyone knows – he doesn't want to spend any extra time with me.

It's so bizarre in the house, everyone is tiptoeing around me, and being careful, yet doing whatever they want when my eyes aren't on them. This is supposed to be a joyous time, the birth of the first grandchild, yet there is this silence that permeates every floor of my parents' house, an eerie hush. There is new life, but it feels like we're sitting shiva.

I stand in the kitchen, sipping my matcha, savoring my moment away from the bedroom upstairs, from the ass-kicking I've been getting as a new mother with a helpless baby. My grandma pores over a news magazine at the table, eating liverwurst on toast with her coffee. I can't imagine wanting to consume that at any time of day, much less as a breakfast. I opt out of sitting down. My mom is stomping around the kitchen, angrily cleaning dishes, fixing things, and putting away food ingredients. My papa disappears, going down to the basement to start work, to escape this scene straight out of *The Royal Tenenbaums*. I can hear Jonah on the phone upstairs, talking slowly and quietly to someone.

It's so weird in this house. *Wes Anderson would be so inspired,* I think.

No one tries to make conversation with me, but as soon as I walk upstairs, they begin talking again. I feel like a pariah. All I want is to be hugged, but I'm so scared that they are contaminated. I want to be held and told that I did a good job, that I am safe, that I am strong.

He never calls his family around me. Every time anyone calls, Jonah shuts himself in my sister's old bedroom, quietly talking for an hour, sometimes showing them the baby, sometimes having them exchange niceties with me. It's so painful. I know he's upset that I don't want anyone traveling to come see the baby before the fourth trimester is over. In countries all over the world, the mother is entitled to a period to cocoon with the newborn, sparing them from outside people, noise, and exposure. It's a forty-day period, where the focus is on taking care of the mama, who takes care of the baby. Not the other way around, where the mama hosts people who want to come see the baby. I want space. I need time to move through the immediacy of postpartum. I need time alone to recover. I need my husband to be with me, to help me recover and come back to myself.

I already felt disrespected, sure that Jonah wouldn't stand up for me with my boundaries and what I want for the baby. Even now, every time I plead with him to do something or not do something, he acts like I've asked him to walk on his hands down to the grocery store. He fumes silently, and I can feel the discord grow. I feel like he is already done with the marriage. Running twenty miles a day to get away from your newly postpartum wife isn't a good sign. I know that. I don't know what happened to the man I fell in love with. I don't even recognize him, but then again, there's no way I recognize myself. I am totally changed, a shell of who I was before pregnancy.

I miss him.

§

We met in 2019, months before the pandemic hit, at a mutual friend's pseudo-Christian gathering. This friend was connected to me through the nonprofit where I worked and had invited me to join him and his friends for an evening of healing and sharing, in typical LA fashion. I showed up with my friend and roommate at the time, Derek, who everyone thought I was dating, but who I, mistakenly, assumed was gay. We had become friends in New York, auditioning for some Broadway musical together, cramped in the 42nd Street Pearl Studios. When I left for Los Angeles, he followed, moving into the micro apartment above my cousins' garage in Inglewood with me, where the rent was a mere $800 a month.

Derek went with me everywhere. That night, we sat together and waited for the event that I had persuaded him to come with me to begin. There was one chair still empty, and as someone started chanting, the door opened. I could see the light of a cigarette being flicked to the ground, ashes settling like dust under the incandescent lighting.

A guy walked into the room, and I caught my breath. He was beautiful – his face so exquisitely handsome it looked perfectly designed, like the Fibonacci sequence was living in his features. His eyes were big and blue, soulful, with long, dark eyelashes, and his lips were enormous, like the kind all women wished they had. Like the ones I had gone to purchase for myself at Kylie Jenner's aesthetician's office the month before. His eyebrows were intense, and almost ran off the sides of his face. I remember thinking he might have been the most beautiful man I'd ever seen. He slouched a bit, moving through the space with swagger, but almost apologetically at the same time.

My future husband took his seat, and I leaned over to Derek. "Who is THAT?" I whispered loudly.

He didn't know.

I stared at the newcomer, taking him in. He had scuffed cowboy boots, long Wrangler jeans, and an Astros jersey. All this, with a backward baseball hat.

I melted.

He was so shy. He didn't talk the entire night, except to introduce himself. Our mutual friend talked for him, letting us know that he came from Texas, his name was Jonah, and his parents were getting divorced. He grimaced when the last part was revealed. The introduction felt more like an AA meeting than the pseudo-culty evening it was supposed to be.

We became friends, not close, but comfortable together. We spent a weekend at Lake Arrowhead with our group – or was it a cult – him quietly sitting on the sidelines, talking softly and just observing. I was loud and flirty, always in a tiny bikini, anorexic, starving for attention and love. He once drove me to my car in a pinch. I'm sorry to say that I never really thought about pursuing him, but maybe we wouldn't be together now if we had dated then. I wasn't in a good space, and he wasn't either. I also felt like he could see through my shtick, and I almost felt intimidated. I was a sad mess, and he was a decent guy. When he left for Texas during the pandemic, I didn't reach out. I was too wrapped up in my own selfishness at that point. I even ghosted him on social media every time he reached out.

It was only when he was living in his van and I moved back from traveling in Spain did we get close. I had been back in Colorado only a week when he messaged me, telling me he was making his way around the Southwest in a van and was in my home state. He wanted to hang out. I ignored the message, but after he messaged me a few more times, I told him to come over the next day, not knowing he was sleeping in his car during a December freeze and had no heat.

When he came over the next morning, my parents told him to park the van in front of the house. We drank Assam tea in the kitchen, laughing and catching up. He sat at the kitchen island, charming and polite with my parents and sister, who had already met him once before. As evening approached, my parents suggested I take him with me to a salsa evening at the ballroom center that night with my friends. He drove us in his van, and I ditched him to go dance, leaving him on the edge of the room. While I danced, he unintentionally met my friends, eventually making the mutual connection. I was so caught up in myself that I forgot to introduce them. He was patient with me and gave me the benefit of the doubt.

When he drove me home, my parents told him to stay parked outside our house. That night, when it got increasingly cold, my mom went and knocked on the door to his van, telling him to come inside to sleep. He ended up curling up on a mountaineering pad in the TV room for a month. We've been together ever since.

We spent every day together, walking miles, talking, saving money on gas and food by ordering hot water at restaurants and cheap food. My sister had us work as actors in her college movie project, pretending to be strangers at a bus station who fall in love over time. There was something in that footage she took – almost a shy longing you could see on both our faces.

I started feeling something pulling me to Jonah. I'm not sure if it was his candor or humor, but it was intoxicating. He listened to me, let me sit in the spotlight, and shine. He was genuinely interested in my life and made me laugh more than anyone else. At this point, he looked like Jesus, with sun-bleached brown hair down his back, a huge beard, and a tan. My parents to this day describe the man that showed up on the doorstep as an outdoorsy messiah. He was muscular and quiet and made me feel seen. The problem was that I couldn't read him. He would awkwardly hug me goodnight, and I tried to get a sense of how he felt, but it was damn near impossible. One day we walked all the way downtown and sat in a Häagen-Dazs and talked about what we wanted in a partner. We both wanted honesty. Neither of us wanted to mess around anymore, I wanted kids. He was open to it.

He finally kissed me after we watched *The Greatest Showman* on my parents' couch one night. He held the back of my neck and leaned in with such conviction, it took my breath away. I felt this settling in my stomach, almost as if my gut was telling me that this was safe, that this is what it was supposed to feel like.

A week later, I left for Texas with him in his van. My parents were so upset, berating me for upending my life. They had different plans for me, but my life was mine alone, and I took a different route than what had previously been imagined for me.

Jonah introduced me to red dirt country music and loved when I slept on his chest. We stayed at his family's lake house in Coldspring, our days spent dancing to slow, romantic music and watching Judd Apatow movies. He told me he loved me early, the words accidentally slipping out one evening in the car. I said it back to him. It felt so organic. I loved how he made me feel, and I couldn't get enough of his smell. We decided to move to Nashville together and got engaged exactly one year after we started dating. Everyone said it was fast, but because we both knew that's where we were going anyway, why prolong the inevitable? We loved each other. We didn't want to be with anyone else. And most of all, we felt safe together.

He accepted me for all the parts that I hated about myself, all my insecurities, all my wounds. I didn't feel self-conscious with him about my eye, my birth defect that I believed would prevent me from finding true love. He proved me wrong, kissing my eyelids, and telling me I was beautiful every day, even when I didn't believe it myself. As cliché as it sounds, he was my person. I still believe he is.

§

Things took a dark turn. Less than a year after getting married, the metaphorical clouds darkened. Now the eye contact we make is anything but tender, and our marriage is tempestuous, at best.

We start to say, "Fuck you". The first time it happens, I am shocked, silent. I am still bleeding from the stitches after I tore during labor, and I have a bladder infection on top of that. The antibiotics that my doctor gives me make me have night terrors, where I wake up, searching the bed for the baby, almost screaming from the panic. The drugs elevate my anxiety, bringing the fear to new heights. Jonah calls me crazy, and when we start fighting, he flips me off and tells me to go fuck myself. My arms drop to my sides. It is bad enough being the woman who isn't respected or cared for postpartum. It's worse being maltreated and spoken to like that.

I want to rip my pants off and show him the stitches, scream at him, reminding him what I gave up, what I sacrificed, what I did to bring a baby into the world with him. I want to fall to my knees, Christlike, begging him to love me again.

Because, I reason, there's no way in hell he can love me and treat me like this.

He's losing weight, fast. Jonah looks like he's been in an internment camp. I know he's only eating candy and diet soda and the occasional taco plate from Torchy's, but I don't want to mother him. I'm struggling enough as a mother. I also feel intense resentment toward him.

How dare you, I think every time he smiles and cuddles our baby. *How can you be sweet to him that much and show me no love at all?*

I feel like garbage – just the vessel for the baby. I feel like Offred in *The Handmaid's Tale*.

They say that women never forget how they are treated when they are pregnant or postpartum, that the experience is so etched into our psyches that it lives on in our bodies long after the baby is grown. The way I was simultaneously ignored and ridiculed is something that I know will take years to mend. I was fearful I would never be able to forgive him if we came out the other side. I didn't know how mean he could be, and I didn't know I had what it took to make him feel small and insignificant.

I am controlling every tiny thing that he does, from making him shower every time he comes back to the house, to washing his hands with burning water and Dawn soap to remove any contaminants. I have stripped him of his dignity, emasculated him, controlled him to the point of being cruel. He complies, but I can see how much he detests everything I tell him to do. I guilt him constantly, shouting that he doesn't care enough about keeping Matias safe. At the time, I truly believed this.

§

We're fighting one afternoon, me in the bathroom at the foot of the stairs, him in the bedroom. He stands up and moves to the doorframe to be able to hear me better as I'm brushing my teeth in the bathroom, careful not to get any toothpaste on my hands. *Who knows what fluoride could do to the baby if he gets it in his mouth.*

I walk back into the room and see that the pillow is over Matias's face. In reality, the pillowcase corner is over his nose, but to me, it's as if I'm walking in on a gruesome scene. Intrusive images shoot through my brain: paramedics coming to try to revive him, me dragging myself down the stairs before hurling myself onto the gurney, bawling, ready to die.

Matias is okay. I check his pulse, hold him to me a second before placing him in the bassinet, and turn on Jonah.

"Fuck you, fuck you, what the fuck is wrong with you?! You could have killed him – you asshole, you have one job! One job!"

I'm yelling and sobbing. *I carried him for nine months, kept him safe, suffered to bring him into this world, and you can't even WATCH him correctly to keep him alive?!* I'm wringing my hands, tears falling down my face onto my white wifebeater tank top I ordered on Amazon – my uniform these days.

Jonah simply says, "I hate you."

I stop. I think my heart stops for a minute. No one has ever said that to me before. Here I am, a new mother, milk pouring out of my boobs, uterus still healing, being told I am hated. In that moment something breaks. There's a crack, a ping, a thud. Something is different and feels like it always will be. It's very hard to come back from that.

I slowly and silently get into bed. Jonah rushes out of the room and starts to pack his things. He says he's done. He wants a divorce. I stay in bed, knowing that this isn't the first or last time he will threaten to leave me.

That's what you want, he always says. *Then you can take the baby. He'll be yours.*

He knows what happens when someone mentions the topic of custody. I start shaking, hyperventilating, my teeth chattering for the umpteenth time this week. I'm suddenly back in the hospital postpartum, with an IV still in my arm. He's reminding me of that trauma that I still haven't processed. It's living in my throat, unable to move down and out of my system. It's sour, like the feeling after you suck on a lemon drop.

§

After Matias was born, I couldn't pee. The nurses tried everything, from peppermint essential oil in the toilet to running the faucet in the sink to get me to release my bladder. It wasn't working. I was pushing hard, too hard, in fact.

Honey, you need to pee, otherwise we will have to insert a catheter.

I feel like they think I'm not trying hard enough.

I shook my head, loose braids shaking back and forth. I hadn't taken them out after giving birth six hours ago, and they were falling out like Pippi Longstocking's braids after a long day. The mint green hospital gown was pulled up around my thighs, and I was sitting on the toilet with two nurses in front of me. They were talking about having to use a catheter, and I knew what that meant, and I didn't want a little tube going back up into my urethra, especially not after just having given birth. *Fuck no, fuck no.*

It ended up needing to happen. I lay back on the recovery bed, Jonah next to me, Matias in the little clear bassinet to my left. I felt traumatized already from the delivery, and now I had to do something that hurt like a motherfucker, just as the epidural had worn off. Jonah averted his eyes but held my hand. It was warm and familiar. He was there for me at that moment. During our son's birth, he showed up emotionally – the glimmer of the personality I loved appeared for those twenty-four hours when I most needed it. I shit on the table, and he didn't even wince. He just stood there, watching the miracle of birth before his eyes while my mom put lavender essential oil in a diffuser, bustling around the room, annoying everyone.

In the morning, my colostrum came in, saffron yellow droplets of liquid gold. I fed Matias, and he gingerly sucked at my boobs. It hurts. I didn't expect to hurt so much with nursing but apparently hurting and nursing are synonymous. It felt like a koi fish was going to town on my chest, and it was hard to believe that my child wasn't born with a full set of teeth. Biting with only gums still doesn't feel good.

I reclined on the bed, drinking my first coffee. It tasted good, but I couldn't enjoy it because I was so tired. My mom came into the room bearing bagels, cream cheese, and other pastry items. She told me she found Jonah asleep, cowboy boots up on a coffee table, passed out cold with candy wrappers all over his stomach. She showed me a picture, and I laughed. Fantastic. Both of us were walking zombies, since the night before we were so scared that Matias was going to die of SIDS that we stayed up all night. I slept for one hour, and Jonah for one hour. The rest of the time we sat, staring at him intently, checking his breathing every twenty seconds. We watched the clock lazily tick as the long night passed by. We called the nurses at least ten times, paranoid about every little thing from the baby's bowel movements to his vomiting up neon green fluid.

Jonah drank a Mexican Coke, and in the middle of the night, my IV still in place, I knocked the glass bottle over. It shattered, shards scattering across the floor, dangerously close to the bassinet.

I lost my shit.

I started screaming at Jonah, guilting him for being so utterly careless.

"What the fuck? Now he's going to die, how could you be such an idiot? What the fuck were you thinking? Some of the glass probably made it into the bassinet. Fuck, fuck, FUCK!"

He didn't yell back at me, but whispered as loudly as he could that the nurses were going to bust into the room and see how crazy we were acting. He made a gesture to show me that I needed to calm down. That made me even more mad. Before he could protest, I pointed at the floor. He glared at me, and got down to pick up the shards, delicately collecting each piece from the linoleum.

"Go in the bathroom, Nola. I got this."

I started crying, shoulders heaving under my hospital gown, stuck to the ground, unable to move. The glass was everywhere, and I was sure that we had put our baby's life in peril.

"Go, now."

I jumped over the mess and went to the bathroom. I couldn't even focus on Matias. Crying, I looked in the mirror.

"Who the fuck are you?" I said to my reflection in the glass.

What stared back at me scared me. I didn't look like the glowing maternity photos I saw on the internet of moms holding their babies after delivery, faces made up, diamonds in their ears and a Hermès bag on the hospital bed. No, I looked like the scene in *Ace Ventura* when he's cosplaying as a mental patient at the psych ward. My whole face was red, fat, and gross. I felt so disgusted with this version of me. I felt sorry for her. She looked feral.

While my mom made me a bagel and sliced it on the counter, one of the postpartum nurses came in to check my vitals. She sat me down on the bed after giving me another Ibuprofen, pulling a folder full of paperwork and flyers out from behind her. My mom handed me the bagel and then left to grab a cup of tea in the cafeteria. The nurse and I were now alone. I bit into my stale sesame bagel.

"Nola," she said, "I know you mentioned during labor that you have obsessive-compulsive disorder."

Shuffle, shuffle of papers.

I shook my head to affirm that yes, I do, and yes, I did mention that. She put her fingers on her lips and raised her eyebrow.

"Do you know what psychosis is?"

She thumbed the papers again, and I looked at her, really looked at her. She was too pretty to be around new mothers. She obviously hadn't gone through the "trial by fire" yet, my new name for pregnancy. She asked me again if I knew what psychosis was. All I could think of was *America's Most Wanted*. I nodded.

"Yes, I know what psychosis is. I wasn't born yesterday – my son was."

"Oh, good. So, you know. Well, I have to talk to you about this –"

She paused as Jonah walked back into the room, looking brain-dead. She motioned for him to join us, and he sat on the chair next to my bed. He looked confused. She began to loop him in, telling him what psychosis was. He didn't know. I wanted to be mean about it, but I refrained.

"Nola has OCD. Because of this," she said, while motioning to my body, "she is at a higher risk of psychosis. You need to watch for the following signs..."

She named them, prattling on about paranoia, bizarre behavior, triggering words, etc.

I wanted to throw up. *What the fuck!* I'd relayed extremely personal and vulnerable information when I was giving birth, and now this woman was telling me I was going to hurt myself and/or my child? At this point I dissociated, fully out of my body. I watched as my soul rose above the bed, looking down at the absolutely traumatized new mother, the nurse telling her she was an unfit mother, and the husband listening intently to the nurse, asking her about what signs he needed to look for. I felt like a wild animal that they were discussing treatment plans for, something that needed to be tranquilized, observed and caged. I imagined my baby being taken out of my arms and handed to CPS, or to Jonah with a divorce lawyer, me being put into a safe house to make sure I didn't hurt my child with my fear of toxoplasmosis, measles, glass, or pigeon poop.

"Nola, Nola."

They looked at me, and I blinked. The nurse wanted me to sign some paperwork. I wanted to punch her in the face. I wanted to scream at Jonah for entertaining her and practically taking notes. I felt paranoid, like he wanted to make sure I could be a mother, and he didn't just need to single-parent our son. I lay down, still outside my body, exactly like I used to do as a little girl. This was too much. I wasn't even twelve hours postpartum, and this all was laid on me. I wanted to scream. I wanted to scream at this woman for taking this delicate moment from me and twisting it into something dark and bad.

My mom returned, steaming Assam tea in hand, Jonah

explained what the nurse had said. My mom silently shook her head, pursed her lips, and went out in the hallway. I heard her through the door, using strong language, berating the nurse for humiliating and scaring the shit out of a new and vulnerable mom. She was giving her that New York business, letting her know she had gone too far.

I curled into the fetal position on the mussed sheets, sleepy, apathetic, and broken.

Sometimes, a girl needs her mom.

Chapter Eight: **Therapy**

We're sitting in the living room of a therapist my mother knows. Our catastrophic conflict has come to a head, and so, for the sake of my mother's sanity and ours, she has called the one woman she believes can fix us.

The breaking point came when Jonah said he's ready to get a divorce, for real, and then ran into the snow outside at five p.m. in a pair of shorts, a short-sleeved shirt, and some gloves. My dad ran upstairs after the door slammed, demanding to know what the fuck was going on. I calmly told him that my husband was going to leave.

"Uh no, that's not going to work."

My dad's brow furrowed, and he called Jonah on the phone, telling him he needed to come back. Now.

Twenty minutes later, my mom, my dad, Jonah, and I met in the living room. Jonah's face is beet red from running outside, his legs sickly white. His blue eyes look huge. He's uncomfortable and looks like he has been crying. I am sitting on a chair pushed back into the kitchen, holding Matias on my chest, thankfully asleep. Thank God he doesn't have to see this shit. My God. I feel so embarrassed, but I feel even more embarrassed for Jonah. I look at him, and he looks like he's going to implode standing there in his in-laws' living room. The shame is palpable. I realize I've never seen this look on his face before. He's ashamed.

My dad acts as a mediator. My mom is glaring at everyone except my dad, obviously furious. She looks over at me to check on the baby.

"He's fine," I say.

"So," my dad begins, "Jonah, it's been brought to my attention that you want to leave, no?"

Jonah shifts his weight, unsure of how to proceed. He puts his hands behind his back, looking in pain.

"Yes, sir. I feel like that is the best thing for me to do. It's not working, and this is not a good environment for anyone."

He lowers his eyes. My dad scoffs and crosses his arms.

"You made a promise. You made a promise to stick by Nola, when you got married. And she made that same promise to you. That isn't just something easily broken. That is a serious commitment. You committed to being by her side through sickness and health, no matter the ups and downs. Did you not?"

Jonah looks down. He's crying. He lets the tears fall. I start crying, and I look and see that my mom is tearing up. This is all terribly sad. And my worst nightmare all at once – my parents confronting my husband, getting an intimate view into our messiness. It feels horrid. My heart is in my stomach, and I feel like I could die sitting there. I am beyond humiliated.

"You're right. I know. I just think – I just think it's better if I leave. I have said horrible things to your daughter," Jonah replies.

He looks at me, and I can feel my cheeks burning. This is

too much. I also said horrible things to him. He tells me that it's not the same. I am postpartum. I didn't and don't deserve that. He is deeply ashamed and deeply sorry. My parents listen with me. I speak a little, but not much. I also apologize to all three of them for being a dictator, for having made micromanagement an art form, for having held them hostage for months while I spiraled, spinning down into my mental illness.

Jonah looks at me, crying more now, his chest heaving. I don't know if he's ever cried like this. My parents watch us. My dad is calm, cool. My mom addresses my husband.

"Jonah, we want you guys to work. We want your marriage to work. We wouldn't be trying to help you if we didn't love you and if we didn't want our daughter to be married to you. We love you, and we know how difficult the first year of marriage is. No one talks about it, but it's true. And Nola is struggling. She didn't ask for this mental illness. She needs you and your support. All she needs is your presence and gentleness. This is just worse than most. Your marriage is worth it. You are worth it."

She stands up and goes to him. Jonah is still bawling, tears cascading onto his T-shirt, his lips blue from the cold, his face crestfallen. My mother hugs him, holds him. He reminds me of a baby bird.

Then my dad turns on me.

"Nola, how can you change to improve your relationship? How can you take accountability?"

I burn. I'm mad. This isn't about me. This isn't about my accountability. I have a mental disease. No part of this is my fault. He's just on his moral high horse.

"What do you mean? That it's my fault? I have OCD. I didn't ask for this! It's a monster. I am not responsible for anything I say – it's OCD talking, not me."

My face is red, and my ears are turning hot.

My dad smiles and shakes his head, disagreeing. He tells me that's not true, that I have practically kept Jonah in a cage of all my fears, controlling his every move, punishing him for not following my every rule.

"You've done the same thing to us," he says.

Jonah is silent. I know they are all wanting me to take some responsibility, but I really don't want to. I don't want to own up to the fact that I've been a living nightmare for everyone and myself. I want to push all the blame on hormones and mental illness. I look at Jonah, though, and I see the pain of someone who has laid it all out on the table, who's tired and full of regret, who hates himself, maybe even more than I hate myself.

"I'm sorry," I murmur. "I'm really sorry too."

The most uncomfortable conversation of my life is over.

§

A week later, we meet Ingrid. She is in her forties, pretty, with a small dog that doesn't know the meaning of personal space. The dog sidles up to the couch and sticks his nose into my crotch. I can't even think about how many OCD violations this causes. He probably has fleas. Or worse, mites.

Ingrid watches me, smiling, while I tentatively touch the dog, feigning comfort. She tells me she knows the dog is bothering me, but asks whether I think I could handle it for a little bit longer. I say okay and move to the other side of the couch. I'll just shower when I get home anyway. No biggie.

Jonah has never been to therapy, and it shows. He grew up thinking therapy equaled failure, and I told him that if that were the case, then I was the biggest failure he'd ever met. I've seen four different therapists since high school, all women, all wildly different. This, though, is very new because Ingrid knows my mom. I don't know if that makes the therapy a waste, but I don't care at this point. I just want someone to help drag us out of this shithole. She seems happy to do it.

Ingrid leans forward and makes eye contact with both of us, crossing her legs.

"Now," she says, "before we begin, there is one question I need to ask – and I want you to both answer honestly."

Ruh-roh. There's no foreplay here. We're not fucking around. Jonah nervously smiles.

"Do you want to be married?"

I look at my husband. His eyes have been perpetually sad since we spoke with my parents. I can see there is love there, but so much self-hatred. It's okay; I hate myself too. Hot take, but I think if you don't hate yourself just a little bit, you're probably an asshole.

"Yes," we both say, almost in unison.

I don't have to think about it. I chose Jonah, and I know I have the autonomy and right to leave him, but I don't want to. We have hurt each other deeply, but I truly think we can get through this. People come back from cheating, people come back from financial ruin. I think we can come back from verbal insults and emotional stonewalling.

§

Over the next few months, I meet with Ingrid three days a week. It drains our bank account, but we figure that if we don't, we won't have a bank account to share. Ingrid comes to us, or I go to her, and she meets Matias. I let her hold him, but I freak out when she rocks him too hard, which in reality is barely at all. She pushes me to do exposures to help my OCD, insisting that in no way am I putting Matias in danger. She's available at all hours, and I take her up on that, sending crazy messages late into the night with whatever is tormenting me – everything from potential spider venom contaminants to the honey in my parents' cupboards.

We discover that Jonah's level of anxiety is off the charts after Matias is born, yet it manifests in ways different from mine. It's hard for me to look at the fact that I probably gave him ninety percent of my anxiety due to my fear mongering. Ingrid challenges him to challenge his issues, and he does his best. We are both struggling, together, and she also reminds us that there is a reason we found each other. We both just have to be on the other's team, as opposed to fighting.

"The issue," she says, "is that you two fight about potentials. What if this happens? What if that happens? Nothing you argue about is actually concrete or substantial. It's all conjecture."

She has a point. I try to change the way I ask Jonah to do

something, and he tries to change the way he responds to it. She tells us about her marriage and about how most people don't talk about the ugly parts of their own spousal relationships. She normalizes marital struggle and helps us look at it from a different perspective, as a chance to grow as people, to change, together.

We start kissing again, although I am scared to let him kiss my face – I think I'll get herpes on my eyes, which he doesn't have, and then go blind. He practices his patience with this, working around my weird compulsions and requests, washing his hands after he touches my butt, since I've developed a whole new issue around fecal matter.

"This is NOT sexy," he laughs. "There is nothing sexy about washing my hands after touching you."

I get sassy, suggesting he wear a hazmat suit, then. He rolls his eyes, but there is a glimmer. He sees me again, and I see him. We don't trust each other yet, but there are moments of affection. We know it's going to take a lot of time – a lot of damage was done.

We band together in the moments when my parents are the ones being obstinate. My mom says she's going to do something I've asked of her, then does something else entirely. She tells me she's taking all the honey out to the garage, yet there it is, still in the pantry, oozing botulism goo around the rims of the jars. My dad makes food and leaves the gas running on the stove with no flame, sending me into a rage in which I call him an idiot, then immediately call two different nurse hotlines.

Jonah and I sit on the bed, taking notes, explaining in explicit detail to the underpaid nurse how long the gas was on, how Matias is acting, and so forth. For a little while, she calms us down.

§

Every time my mom cooks chicken, I have to meditate in my room and do those Scandinavian breathing exercises that I learned in Los Angeles. I am so grossed out and freaked out by salmonella that she banishes me from downstairs around dinnertime, but not before I make her promise on her own life that she will clean the surfaces and utensils within an inch of their lives and that she won't cross-contaminate anything. The water filter hangs over the sink, and I just know there's parasitic raw chicken juice splashing all over the head of the water dispenser. No one should ever eat chicken. It's completely foul.

Ingrid tries to make me overcome the chicken fear, but I refuse.

"That's too much," I say.

She cheerfully tells me how one day I will be able to handle raw meat, no problem. I think she's delusional. Instead of the chicken, she approaches me with the second biggest issue – honey.

From the moment I first read that children under one can't have honey due to the botulism spores that potentially lurk within the sticky stuff, I have avoided it like the plague. It's completely fine to consume it during pregnancy, but I got it into my head that it wasn't – that there was probably some microscopic chance that it could cross the placenta.

§

Ingrid takes me to the neighborhood coffee shop. I haven't been in one since I was three months pregnant, and I feel like an alien who has come down to earth and is now experiencing human life for the first time. I feel strange and janky as I order an iced latte and a pistachio croissant. She stands next to me and points out a woman with her baby, sitting on the floor. I can't help but think of how irresponsible that looks. I'd never do that. I would never expose my baby to all those potential contaminants and germs. There are probably chemicals on the floor, at best. The baby puts her fingers in her mouth, and I shiver.

My therapist looks like my caretaker, and I look horrible, I'm sure. I'm wearing jeans that are at least two sizes too tight, flip-flops, and a purple, moth-eaten cashmere sweater that I think was my mom's in the eighties. I didn't brush my teeth this morning, either. When the coffee comes and they call our names, I notice a honey dispenser sitting on top of the espresso machine. I'm sure that the man who made my coffee rubbed his hands all over it before touching my cup, and I grab a tissue before touching my drink. I wrap it around the outside of the sweating plastic cup, using my hair tie to secure it. Then I take my handy little hand sanitizer out of my pocket, squirt a bit on my hands, and rub this all over the outside of the cup too, even the mouth hole. *Chas v'shalom* I end up with herpes from a barista.

Ingrid is watching me this entire time and then ushers me toward the door. I spend the next thirty minutes of our walk asking for her honest opinion on whether or not my pastry might have honey in it.

"It doesn't matter, Nola – you aren't feeding Matias spoonfuls of honey. He isn't going to die from botulism."

I'm not convinced. I know that in Orthodox Christianity, babies are christened in the first few months by being doused in holy water, then given a teaspoon of honey, to represent the sweetness of life or something. I wonder how many of those babies contract botulism, and if Greece or Russia has huge surges of infant mortality due to this. I mention it to Ingrid, and she shakes her head and puts her face in her hands. She touches her mouth for a moment, and I ask her to wash her hands when she gets back to our house. I don't want her touching Matias after touching her lips – that's how you contract HSV-1. She complies. She's used to this shit. It's her job.

§

We find out that we are being transferred to Sitka for Jonah's new job, to a tiny island scattered somewhere on the tail of Alaska. We watch *The Proposal* to prepare for the move, volume turned down as low as possible so we don't "burst the baby's eardrums." It looks beautiful, and Ryan Reynolds makes it look even better, but after looking into the movie on Wikipedia, I find out they filmed it in Connecticut. *What the fuck – why?* Jonah mentions something about weather and rainfall, and I shrug it off. At least it would be isolated, and I don't have to interact with anyone. I want to live in a bubble if I can. It actually sounds nice.

All hell breaks loose ten days before we are supposed to leave my parents' house for Alaska. My mom invites her friend and his entire family into the house. Matias is barely two months old and doesn't have all his vaccines, and measles is running rampant. Jonah comes up from the garage to tell me they are all in the driveway and my mom is embracing them. At this point, I'm not letting anyone in the house to see Matias, so afraid am I of COVID, whooping cough, and the flu.

"Babe, they could be coming into the house..." He trails off, waiting for my response.

"She wouldn't. There's no way."

I stiffen, hearing the sound of voices less than twenty feet from my safe baby, peacefully sleeping. I can't believe it. We made sure Jonah's parents were up to date on their Tdap vaccine before coming here, and now she is letting in an entire family whose current health and vaccination status we don't know? I'm irate.

The voices taper off after about ten minutes of talking, and I hear my mom say goodbye way too loudly. Jonah gives me a warning look as if to say, *Please be careful,* and I open the door loudly, on purpose, and run halfway down the stairs. My mom looks up at me sheepishly from the kitchen sink, where she's washing fresh basil. She knows she fucked up, and yet she continues making pesto.

"Are you stupid?!" I scream at her.

Chapter Nine: **Mother**

I am a mother now. I can breastfeed while drinking a cold cup of coffee, sticky with maple syrup, while trying to catch up on emails. I can go most of the night with little to no sleep, hyperaware of Matias breathing and Jonah snoring softly. I can light a beeswax candle with my nine-month-old in my arms, as he pulls at my earlobes, or walk the dog with the baby in the carrier while rain pours outside. I can bake banana bread while singing to my little one, who's having a teething meltdown. I can last the entire day without taking a shower, my white cotton shirt soaked through with milk, sour and stained.

I dress Matias in wool and organic cotton because I'd rather have a few nice things for him than a boatload of unhealthy crap. I worry about microplastics and lead, EMFs and fluoride. I dump my closet full of clothing into a bag to give away, wading through dresses I'll never wear, looking for pure textiles and items I never would have bought before. I crave comfort and warmth and security. I give him wooden toys to play with, and German dolls that are Waldorf approved. I listen to podcasts on anthroposophy and Steiner pedagogy, preparing myself for a life spent trying to create a normal childhood for my children, focusing on imagination. I guilt myself if he sees the TV while

I watch something. I watch anyway, needing to keep my sanity.

I speak to my baby in Italian, lulling him to sleep with "Edelweiss," over and over. I lay him on the sheepskin I've had for over fifteen years, watching him intently study the patterns and indentations in the buttery material, before trying, unsuccessfully, to eat it. I give him only healthy food that has been regeneratively farmed. I dream of homeschooling and drawing and painting with him on rainy afternoons, cuddled up on the carpet with our dog. We'll watch monarch butterflies emerge from their chrysalises and dry their dewy wings on the lilacs outside in our garden. Jonah will make us a fire outside so we can watch the aurora borealis in our flannel pajamas with tea outside of our Alaskan home. We'll wake to kids running into our room at six a.m. on Hanukkah and Christmas mornings, snow on their noses as they drag us downstairs to open presents.

Then I am reminded. I live in fear, and it is real and omnipresent and beats me down every day. I may get to experience all of this, but a shadow sits over me. I'm reminded of Michaelmas in ninth grade, learning about St. George and the Dragon. The tale morphed from George killing the dragon to him *taming* the dragon. I never understood the metaphor until now. My teacher showed us a routine with eurythmy, and I remember thinking it was the dumbest thing I'd ever seen. In her soft shoes and German accent, Helga gave us scarves to drape over our backs.

We all have demons, children. We must only learn to tame them. We all have a shadow self that we see every day, hiding behind corners in the space between minutes. Tame your dragon. Hm.

But, Helga, I want to say now, *I have too many. What if I have too many?*

I live with the fear of something awful happening to my baby. I overanalyze every situation, trying to avert a crisis before it shows up, sidestepping catastrophe while trying to maintain my dignity. I'm not graceful in this sense, asking people roundabout questions in order to skirt around being direct with them. All I want to do is yell exactly what I think all the time.

Were your hands one hundred percent clean before you put them in my baby's mouth to check for teeth? You said you washed your bathroom with bleach. BLEACH. You said you showered afterward. But what about the residue under your fingernails? Did you wash them well enough in the past twenty-four hours to get rid of any tiny particles? Why did I even ask you to do this? I try to be normal for one second and it backfires on me. Every. Damn. Time. It's not like you knew, and it's probably totally fine, but still, I want to be sure none of the leftover bleach got inside his mouth or system. Did you scrub well enough when you showered? You said you don't use gloves. That makes me wildly uncomfortable. No gloves with bleach? Don't you worry about it not leaving the bathroom walls and then falling on you when YOU shower? I would never use bleach. Shit. Shit. Shit. Shit.

§

When I wake up in the morning, sometimes these fears diminish; sometimes they won't go away for months on end. Glass, chemicals, pesticides, disease, viruses, germs.

Everything is contaminated. And the worst part is, I can't prevent everything, and I can't be honest. I'm not crazy. I just have an unbalanced fear barometer. I went from reckless maidenhood to careful motherhood in the course of nine short months.

I've been barely coping on this Alaskan island for six months, dealing with the incessant rain and barely going outside. I can't tell night from day, because I almost never go out my front door. My child has never even touched grass, and I feel like that might be illegal. We wait all day for Jonah to come home, and then when he does, I go and take a bath, closing my eyes in the water and letting the Epsom salts do their job.

The transition to Alaskan life takes a toll on all of us, and even though I barely move my body or exert myself, I'm still fatigued. I feel like one of those Victorian women draped across a daybed in the portraits at the Met, sans the beautiful clothing and delicious fruit. I stay in the bath as long as possible, turning into one of the prunes from those ornate paintings, trying to find the motivation to get the fuck out and go make food, smile, dance, laugh, or do anything at all.

Every time we go outside, I tread cautiously, like on eggshells. We live a block and a half from the airport, and I schedule our outings so that we aren't walking when the planes are about to take off. I can't handle the noise that might rupture our baby's eardrums or the smell of jet fuel that could cause SIDS. There is a family that smokes a few doors down, and every time I smell smoke, we rush inside. I strip down in the front hall, peeling my clothes off like they are a biohazard. I make Jonah do the same, and I bathe, then he bathes, then Matias bathes, until I'm satisfied there are no potential particles left. I've already thrown away all my clothes that I ever wore while smoking cigarettes, and I have two pairs of pants and three shirts left. I also tossed everything that *potentially* could have been exposed.

The upside is that there is peace between Jonah and me. We are rebuilding our marriage, gentle with each other, careful not to open old wounds. I am too often punishing him for the postpartum period, getting too comfortable with hurling insults his way. I called him a "pussy ass bitch" once, and he laughed it off.

He tells me he will spend his entire life atoning for how he treated me when Matias was born. That feels nice, and kind of like an insurance policy as well. He hugs me again, and when I am in hysterics with a bout of bad compulsions, he holds my face in his hands, kissing my cheeks and telling me that I'm the best mama. I weep crocodile tears into his chest, careful not to touch my eyes to his shirt.

Matias is starting to notice how we interact with each other, and with other people, so this physical sweetness feels especially important.

When Jonah is on the boats, we track him on my phone, seeing how far he goes on the marine highway system, making sure he comes back when he's scheduled to. Every time he leaves, I say a little prayer, knowing that the dangers of this job are not a joke. It's gnarly, and I can see it on his face, most often when he comes home at night.

I could never do his job. Even just thinking about driving a boat makes me stressed. Especially at night. His hands are starting to bleed and chafe from the wind and cold, like mine used to.

§

As I improve, my new Alaskan therapist, Doug, encourages me through every milestone I reach, the hurdles I hurdle over. He is middle aged, with a face that looks like he has seen things, and I have started referring to him as my Yoda. He is no frills, and doesn't like to cut corners, so every week I must do more exposure therapy. I have succeeded in being able to cook meat, not including chicken. I promise him that will never happen again. I am good going my entire life without poultry again.

On Christmas morning, I wake up at three and take a pregnancy test by myself in our bathroom. It's positive. I smile, ready to do this shit over again. The frantic sex we had in the kitchen after I baked that incredible apple cake worked. We were almost manic at that moment, and I remember thinking, *I'm pregnant.* It's what we wanted – I wanted to have another baby while I still remembered the trenches of pregnancy, the pain of childbirth, and the achiness and depression of postpartum. I wanted to get it out of the way and over with before I forgot how bad it could be. I also knew that sometimes women with perinatal OCD have few to no symptoms with their second pregnancies.

Silly me, thinking my OCD was going to completely disappear this time around. Mental health problems don't just go away. You have to constantly remind yourself that what you're terrified of is an overreaction. It's like having a monkey on your back at all times.

OCD is infuriating because it makes me feel less credible as a mother. Every worry I have is overlooked by those close to me because I'm a chronic worrier. Every request I have is pushed aside because, in their minds, I'm overreacting, even if it's something a lot of moms nowadays worry about. It makes me feel foolish. I'm a diehard people pleaser, or at least I used to be, and I am still nervous about offending people when I ask them not to touch my baby's feet. Dumb, I know. I envy Jonah, who is able to say whatever pops into his head at any time, no matter who it is. He is unabashedly courageous and also foolish in that way. He can stand up for our parenting choices – I can't. I'm calculated, and I overthink every text message. It makes me feel guilty either way, whether I'm offending someone or not standing up for myself. The only solace I have is knowing that these people who judge will someday become parents too and realize how difficult it is to enforce boundaries around your children, even with people you love. They too will understand that it is totally acceptable to ban kissing, and to expect anger from those who are supposed to be there to support you.

I decide I'm not going to let OCD win this time around. I eat bananas and veggies even though my mind goes on an endless loop of toxoplasmosis, listeria, salmonella, *E. coli*–each one flashing through me every time I fork a bite into my mouth. I watch with a kind of envy as I see my pregnant friends online do whatever the fuck they want with a fuck-all attitude. I realize I'm not fun anymore, so I buy synthetic clothing and don't obsess over inorganic fibers. We put Matias to sleep in his own room at a little over a year old, and he cries. It's horrible, but we get our marriage back, now able to watch TV and snuggle together on the couch. I listen to podcasts about parenting from every point on the political spectrum, and if I have to hear one more time how vaccinating my kids makes them autistic, I am going to scream.

I'm doing it differently this time – I'm a modern woman; therefore, I can be a modern mama. And it doesn't make me any less of a mother to feel good about myself.

Chapter Ten: **Roman Empire**

I haven't washed my skin properly in over two years. I lean over the counter, staring at my crusty, dry face. There are discolored patches on my forehead. These make me look old. My hands are so dry and cracked from overwashing and never using hand lotion. I'll occasionally use Aquaphor, but then wash it off, scared that Matias will eat some and then I'll have to call the doctor. My hands are a mess, little cuts everywhere – almost a bad metaphor for how I feel like I'm slowly dying, a death by a thousand cuts. A thousand little pieces of me fractured, sloughing off my body until I'm dust.

But my face. My face looks so damn old. I actually feel disgusted with my appearance, whereas in the past, I've only been mildly appalled, depending on the day. I've picked at the area where I had perioral dermatitis so much that it's now scarred, and I know the only thing that will cure that is some good old-fashioned retinol. No scammy tallow balm is going to help the damage I've done – and my God, how I've tried to make that work.

§

In Oklahoma, I started using tallow balm, trying out the Weston A. Price diet, and dressing like Laura Ingalls Wilder. It didn't stick. The first time I put tallow balm all over my face and got into bed, the dogs ran at me, looking for food. Jonah looked at me, leaned in for a kiss, and said I smelled like a burger.

"It's beef fat!" I explained, exasperated.

"It's WHAT?" Jonah started laughing, unable to believe I'd do that. "Why, Nola, why?"

I started laughing too. Truth be told, I felt like a pig getting ready for the state fair, bathing in buttermilk. It took me days to get the smell off my skin, and I threw the jar out, for good measure.

At this point, I haven't used anything on my face in years.

I turn my chin and try to see how much worse my scleral shell looks now. It's been over six years with the same one, and it's becoming more and more obvious that it's a contact lens and not my actual eye. It needs to be cleaned professionally, and the sheen on it looks cloudy and almost opaque now. Jonah says you can't tell and people don't look, but I know you can, and they do.

My bump is growing, and I casually push against the counter, an action that would've sent me into a tailspin last year. But I know the baby is okay. He's nestled in there, like a bug in a rug. I'm not gaining as much weight as last time, and that's good, my doctor says, after I ended up in the ER last month with a burst varicose vein behind my left knee. Now I've got them in my groin too, and they hurt like a motherfucker. I'm constantly nervous that I am actually anorexic and not eating enough for this baby. What a piece of shit I am if that's the case. Not eating enough so my veins are okay. *What a bitch.*

The mirror is filthy. I notice a red spot on my lip and it starts to feel tingly.

OMG is that a cold sore?

I start to feel panic. There is nothing I am more scared of at this moment during this pregnancy than herpes. It becomes fully psychosomatic, where I lie in bed at night thinking I probably have it and I'm going to transfer it by kissing Matias's head, and then Jonah will get it, and I'll go blind, and the world will be over. I discovered a wart on the knuckle of my middle finger on my right hand while putting Matias to bed the other night.

My heart immediately dropped – now I have to worry about this too. I don't want to pass this on to my babies. Impeccable fucking timing. I have been wrapping a Band-Aid or duct tape around the finger, alternating between the two and wearing down the skin so it looks like I've been in the bathtub for two days. It's gross, but the wart is going to set me off. I can't touch anything if I don't have it covered – it's contagious. I debate the fact that herpes is a lot worse than warts to try to make myself feel a little better.

The intrusive thoughts start pouring in. I'm still homed in on the wart, knowing it could have been passed to me from anyone, and from anywhere. My brain launches into its own soliloquy, and I can't do anything to stop my ranting brain from going down the drain of a panic attack.

I probably got it as a kid because my mother was so fucking irresponsible. Maybe that one hookup in Shanghai. I'm a whore. Maybe the nurse at the OB's office gave it to me. I should sue her ass. If I have herpes, then Matias and the next baby are in danger.

The virus can kill newborns if they get it. There is a couple in Scotland who are raising awareness because their newborn died of the virus, and they don't even know where she got it from. If I gave the virus to anyone, especially a baby, I would just walk in front of oncoming traffic. I can't hold my new baby. OMG, do I need a C-section now? Should I get an antibody test? I heard that 90 percent of people have the virus, even if it is dormant. How will I ever pee again and sit on a public toilet? How do I trust anyone? Life is fucking horrible. God should just wipe us all out and start over. We're all just scabby, infected, contagious messes, procreating and shitting and consuming crap. What is the point?

I start picking at the scabs on my chin, furiously. I grab my phone to try to distract myself for at least five minutes from the cartoon sirens in my head. The internet temporarily makes me not think. I get on Instagram to try to ignore my brain and the overwhelming doomsday thoughts that sidle in. I hop over to Amazon and decide to be a strong woman and fight my fear of skincare and going blind and purchase Cetaphil face wash. *I'm taking back my life! One underwhelming facial wash at a time!*

I put down my phone and stare at myself in the mirror. I'm pathetic. I really want my life back. I want to be able to once again be the person who can sit on the floor of a public bathroom without thinking about all the germs and viruses. I've researched too much for my own good, and I really love and hate Google at the same time. I can tell you how long HSV-1 lives on porous surfaces without thinking twice. I know what disinfectants get rid of what viruses, and I have calculated the rate at which the herpesvirus would die on packages that I order from Amazon. I have this surplus of information that would be useful to maybe someone who works in the medical field, but I don't need to know it. It gives me nothing. It takes away my sleep and my youth and my innocence and my will to go out in the world and be normal. I feel like a freak, and I'm exhausted.

§

Last time I was pregnant, I was very vocal with all my worries. This time, with this baby, I internalize everything and let it bubble below the surface. I'm faking it to appear okay, because I don't want anyone to pity me or think me unfit to be a mother. I don't want anyone talking behind my back, and I certainly don't want anyone trying to parent my children in my place. Squashing down the thoughts seems to be working, at least for the time being. I at least appear as if I have my shit together, even if inside I'm screaming.

I pop open an almost nonexistent pimple to distract myself. Now my hands are dirty, and I probably will get a staph infection or strep on my face and end up going into sepsis.

Breathe in. Breathe out. Breathe in.

I hold my breath. Jonah is downstairs with the baby. I'm supposed to be taking time for myself right now, but it's almost not worth it. I don't even know what to do except binge-watch trash TV or try to read a book or obsessively worry. I can't even decide what to eat for dinner, and now I'm worried about the name I had originally wanted for this baby. It doesn't seem like it fits or flows or something. I second-guess myself. I could also see the option of picking his name after he's born and we're looking at him, but maybe I'll be so conked out on the epidural that I'll suggest something ridiculous like "Quartz" or "Jethro."

§

I keep dreaming that the baby's name is now Rome. Maybe I really miss Italy, or maybe the simplicity of the sounds is appealing. Rome. Rome, Romy, Romi. It's warm, like the name has already been lived in for millennia by historians speaking about it. It works with our last name. It's not quite conventional. It ends with a silent vowel. It works for an adult or a child. It's a conversation starter too.

Yeah, my mom wanted to call me Rome because she kept dreaming of the word and went crazy with perinatal OCD during her pregnancies.

I know I'll tell him and his brother that I only wanted to listen to Tchaikovsky with Matias, and with the second, Shostakovich's waltzes, which I heard for the first time in the *Anna Karenina* movie.

Rome. Maybe, maybe not. Pregnancy has not been my so-called Roman empire. But maybe it has. Maybe this complete breakdown of who I was is, in a way, just that. I feel like a completely different person. Maybe Rome is fresh, new, hopeful. But Romi means "joy." *Is that better? Is that the perfect name for our child?*

§

I get in the car and go to the bookstore on the main street of our tiny town. The resident Corgi, named Peach, wiggles her way over to my feet, and I let her sniff my dirty white tennis shoes. I'm looking for a sign, some sort of inspiration, to tell me what our second son's name should be. I'm careful not to touch the walls with my clothes, lest the pathogens infect my clothing. I don't want to bring home Ebola, for God's sake.

The bookstore is nice. It's quiet and organized – two of my favorite attributes of any person or place. The kids' section has a papier-mâché sky constructed above the books, fluffy white clouds speckled on a blue, blue sky. The women who work there don't get in your business, and the sounds of the espresso machine in the attached coffee shop are comforting. I can smell the beans. The women eye me, raising an eyebrow to suggest that they are there if I need help, but I don't, because I don't even know what I'm looking for. An answer, I guess.

God, please speak to me through the authors' names on these books.

Maybe I need to buy some books on Rome or something. Something pings off my amygdala.

What is a bad connotation with this name?

When we were naming Matias, I looked up convicted criminals to make sure there wasn't anyone crazy famous or deranged with his name. There wasn't, just a bunch of Argentinian soccer players and one burglar in Brazil or something. I had considered the name Roman for him, but then got stuck in my relationship OCD, where my brain convinced me it wasn't okay to name him that because that was the name of a character in

Succession, and I had watched that show for the first time with an ex in Los Angeles. Also, some other people with the name Roman didn't seem so great, Roman Polanski for one. Dumb brain, thinking I was tying my kid to one of the other eight billion people in the world with the same moniker.

Someone coughs, and I freeze. I don't have a mask on – what could they have that would make life infinitely more difficult while pregnant? Strep? Croup? Whooping cough? I sidle up to the poetry section and try to avoid the people walking past me. I rub my belly, comforting Rome or Romi, or whatever his name will be, but knowing it's really just for me. I feel like my OCD is revving up toward the end of this pregnancy. I'm starting to have day nightmares about the baby being switched in the hospital, even though there are three delivery rooms and eight thousand people on the island, and there would be no way all of them would be pregnant and giving birth at the same time.

"It's absolutely ridiculous," Doug says. "Your worry about this is high on the list of craziest things I've heard. Maybe even the craziest."

"Well, maybe now it can be anecdotal to other insane mothers-to-be," I say snarkily.

He laughs at me. It's disarming, but I know it's genuine.

But I can't get it out of my head. I know that it is a ludicrous worry, fueled by my OCD and progesterone, but I don't want to go down the path of mental anguish, delirious in those sweet days of newborn bliss about whether or not the baby I'm holding is mine. I think it might kill me, worrying about that. I'm scared I won't be attached because I'll think he's someone else's

– some other baby while mine is being nursed or bottle-fed by another mother in Sitka. I went on Reddit and went down the rabbit hole of paranoid moms who mark their newborns with a Sharpie or even go as far as to get a DNA test. I suggest this to Jonah, but he says it's cruel to make him be in pain to satisfy my scared thinking pattern. I remind him that he wanted to get him circumcised, which is way more invasive and a lot more painful. He walks quickly into the kitchenette to avoid getting in a fight. He says I use my intellect to fight dirty.

The bookstore is empty now, except for me and the globe I'm carrying out in front of me. I see stock paper in different colors on the shelf, and I fantasize about making a sign to carry around my neck while out with my newborn. It would say, *DON'T KISS MY BABY* in block lettering, for emphasis.

"When are you due?" the woman at the counter asks me. I look at her mouth, to check for herpes.

"Not soon enough," I say.

She laughs awkwardly. I don't see anything on her lips, just lip gloss.

"No, seriously, though, I'm due in a month."

She smiles.

The travel books are on the back wall. I finger through the jackets, looking for "Italy." I find the *Lonely Planet* guide on Rome. Flipping through jettisoned pictures of *cacio e pepe* pasta and the Spanish Steps fills the pages, already full of tiny print. I stop for a minute and feel the tears welling up in my eyes.

I wish I could become who I was.

I hide my face even more in the book, now openly crying,

albeit silently. *Fuck my brain.* That person who lived there, who traveled to Rome to see two popes speak, by train – I'm mourning her. She was alive, well, spontaneous, and vivacious. I'm anything but. It's a big deal for me to walk through a bookstore, and the memories I have of being in cities full of people hugging and kissing are alive only in my mind. I wore dresses and thongs, hair down. I smoked cigarettes sometimes, and sometimes not. I rolled my own cigarettes, my feet tucked under me on the balcony, flicking the ashes into the lavender plants. I drank house wine at lunch, filling up on bread before the *primo piatto* because life was meant to be lived. I laughed with my mouth open. I was inspired and open to anything.

I want my boys to live like that. I want them to be free, I don't want to be the person they talk about in therapy who made them neurotic and held them back from what life can actually be. I fucking hate myself now. I'm a mother now, exactly what I felt called to do and excited for, and then my brain short-circuited, and I can't enjoy the actual mothering part. I love caring for my toddler as well as for this little guy in my belly, but I feel pangs of anger, perhaps, at the genetics at play in all of this. At least we won't have girls who will get perinatal OCD as well. At least my boys are spared from that.

Chapter Eleven: **Different, but the Same**

I give birth to him, and I give him the name Rome practically as we're walking out of the hospital. I couldn't decide, indecisive and unsure of myself as I always have been. I kept going between the strength of the name Rome, and the joy of the name Romi. I ask the doctor's opinion, and she suggests sticking with Rome. She tells me this just as we're about to go in for the circumcision, me clutching the still-nameless baby, following her into the miniature operation room. I know she thinks this is an OCD meltdown, as she's been dealing with my shenanigans for months as her patient. She's patient, but she's tired.

I ask other people too, and they agree. It sounds more mainstream – Romi, according to them, sounds too young and not masculine enough. I don't like that answer. I still love the name Romi, no matter what anyone says. I love Rome too, but I can't decide, and even as I am forced to leave the hospital, I feel unsure while writing the name. I check my pulse to see if it feels right, but I've taken so many rounds of Tylenol and ibuprofen that I don't even know how to get back to the car. How was I supposed to pick the right name while in such a delirious state?

Labor and birth this time are euphoric, cathartic even, as they redeemed all of my hopes for what birth was supposed to be. It felt like a renaissance for me as a mother, and perhaps that's why I decided to name him Rome Leni – strength and light. I could tell that people weren't psyched about the name I chose. I also still love Romi. Rome is monosyllabic, assertive, determined – a little gladiator.

Our difficult-to-name baby was born at 10:14 p.m. on a warm night in August, earlier than his due date. I curb-walked for an hour as I ate a croissant that morning, confident that I would be giving birth that day. By the time I got my epidural, I was having serious contractions and had eaten my weight in lime green Jell-O. My doctor went home to have dinner with her family and then came back to deliver the baby. I was shaking, and my legs were hurting like they never had, my varicose vein swollen and irritated from the sheer force of the contractions. I didn't want to watch TV or listen to anything. I just wanted to stare at nothing and sit in silence. Jonah paced around the delivery room, sipping on black coffee and making sure I was comfortable, supplying me with a steady stream of Sprite to keep my blood sugar up, especially when the epidural put me into such a state that I nearly passed out. I started to feel dizzy, then laid my head back, telling Jonah I just needed to sleep for a little bit. He alerted the nurses and made sure they checked on me.

"That epidural hit me like a train," I said between sips of soda.

Both times I've given birth, I've been completely quiet. I internalize my pain and vocalize my anxiety. I realized before I started pushing that I was really scared. I was still ultra-paranoid about losing sight of the baby, and having him be switched at birth with someone else. Jonah told me this was ridiculous for two reasons – one, this was Sitka, and there were more nurses here than women giving birth, and two, the probability of a woman giving birth to a baby at the same time, one who looked similar to me and whose baby was also a boy, was, in fact, extremely unlikely.

I didn't listen to him, sure that if it was going to happen, it would happen to us. I told him he needed to watch the baby like a hawk, and every time I went to pee, to have all eyes on him, just in case a nurse tried to do a switcheroo.

The nurses all turned out to be incredibly accommodating and sweet, not treating me like a freak when I told them I was more mentally unstable than usual.

The sun went down, and when I was ready to push, all the intrusive thoughts and visions popped into my brain. I paused, and looked at Dr. F.

"You're struggling, aren't you, Nola? Don't believe the stories you are telling yourself, lady. You got this, mama."

In that moment, I loved her. She patted my foot and refocused on my nether regions, speaking to the nurse beside her, prepping me to push this baby out. The nurses had marveled at how much the little guy was moving – the epidural made him go even crazier, pushing his limbs up into my ribs and staying there until I could barely catch my breath. Jonah looked at me, his hand on my knee.

"He's a wild one," he said.

I lay my head back and put my hands over my eyes.

"I am capable. I am strong. I am a mother," I whispered to myself.

Dr. F looked at me, realizing that I was absolutely ready to have this baby born into the world. I wouldn't push the three hours that I had pushed the time before, fearful of having my cornea detach. This was the real deal, and I was ready to become my own version of a Tiger Mom, not scared anymore, just fierce and protective. She signaled to the nurses that I was ready.

Jonah was the only man in the room when I delivered. It felt liberating, almost primal, to be surrounded by women as I pushed our second baby into the world. Through the first pushes, I thought of *The Red Tent*, the book in which nomadic Jewish women gather to menstruate, celebrate, grieve, and give birth.

This was my red tent.

The energy was lighter, faster, and more exciting than when Matias was born. I was seasoned and knew what to expect. I was ready to push, to let go and believe in my body and my baby. I pushed for only seventeen minutes, and then Romi arrived, screaming into the Alaskan night. I felt energized, like someone had dumped a bucket of water over my head. He was vivacious, strong, ready to be earthside. I looked up at Jonah. He was holding my hand, and he pushed his glasses onto his forehead, crying. I smiled and cried as well, as Dr. F put our baby on my chest, his little naked body warm. The energy in the room was warm, the love between me and Jonah was warm. It was as it was always supposed to be – just us, experiencing the miracle of the new life we brought into the world, with the most important thing: *our* love.

To top it off, I didn't poop on the table.

Jonah and I stared at this new little bean. The hurt, the pain, the struggle that we endured and that we put each other through seemed to melt in that moment. We landed. We redeemed ourselves, as parents and as partners, for the second time. Jonah leaned over me and kissed me. He told me he loved me, and he was so happy. I lay back on the hospital bed and closed my eyes as Romi ate for the first time. I was home.

§

The next morning, I got to see his little face in the light for the first time. Jonah photographed us in the dappled sunlight of the glorious August morning, me in my standard men's white tank top, the baby wrapped in my arms and nursing hungrily. In the photos, I am smiling up at Jonah with my eyes squinting – I don't have my contact lens in. My hair is in a messy bun, and my Magen David hangs around my neck, askew, the gold chain my grandma gave me glittering in the sunrays. I feel like Athena, like I could do anything. I am woman, hear me roar.

I sit in the hospital room all day, my mom at home with Matias, eating Italian food from the only restaurant down the street. Jonah serves me a container full of gigantic meatballs, and my favorite, Caesar salad. It all feels very Dionysian, and I want someone to dim the lights and put on some Frankie Avalon. I wanted a Roman meal, something in tune with the energy this baby brought into the world – boldness and a kind of loving ferocity.

He's hungry all the time and giving me absolutely no time

to sleep. I rest between feeding frenzies, while Jonah stands and rocks the baby overlooking the mountains outside. My body is so tired, and I put on my compression socks to help the swelling in my legs.

§

When we go home, Matias won't have anything to do with me, and I feel depressed again. When Jonah brought him to the hospital, he was so unsure, so very confused about the noisy little bundle on my lap, nursing from his mama, taking all his mama's attention. He was shy, and I immediately felt guilt for having left him for a night. *How dare I,* I thought. *He's going to be so fucked up after this. I should've given birth at home.*

He ignores me for about two weeks, and in that time, I wander aimlessly through the house with a massive diaper on, bleeding onto the witch hazel pads. It's not my first rodeo, but it doesn't mean it's any prettier. I bleed through the sheets and only want to watch old comedy specials, laughing along to John Mulaney's antics while the new baby lies on my chest. The sun stays up until eleven at night, and between that and the constant feeding, I never sleep.

My mom cooks for me, and Jonah takes Matias to do things together, to ease him into his new role as a brother. I have a brief panic attack when I realize I went to the bathroom and left Romi alone in the room on Day 2 at the hospital, and I start to think that maybe someone switched him with another baby. Jonah and my mom both have to talk me down from that ledge, my postpartum rage boiling, me in hysterics as I think I broke my own rule and would have to suffer the consequences. It's exhausting and embarrassing being batshit crazy when those hormones drop.

§

When my mom leaves, we have to juggle taking care of two kids for the first time, and we get even less sleep. At no point are either of us resting, and Romi is so demanding that I am feeding him at all hours of the day, for only a few minutes at a time, until he is satisfied.

My rage starts growing. I start to get frustrated with Jonah over tiny things – dishes in the sink, clothes left on the floor, a cup that spilled. He tells me it doesn't matter, we're in the trenches here. But to me, it matters. A lot. Losing my temper becomes easy, and I get too comfortable getting angry with him. I feel like I am entitled to it because of what happened during the last postpartum period. I know I shouldn't, but I use it as leverage. The difference is that he has learned patience, and when I start to get mean, he says that he needs to take a break and walks into the next room to breathe. I easily get into a circuitous loop, where I go around and around until someone helps me to get off the hamster wheel and look at things from another perspective.

This time around, Jonah is determined to react differently, to listen and use the mediation techniques that we learned with Ingrid.

On the other hand, Doug is now ever-present in my life,

knowing from his own experience of having children that the second time around isn't necessarily easier. We talk ad nauseam about all of my triggers, him suggesting some entry-level exposures to get ahead of the game on my fears. I agree to try.

§

The first one I agree to attempt is to try having some honey.

It's been over two years since I have had any, and the mere thought of the stuff heightens my cortisol and makes my blood pump faster. Knowing that this exposure therapy will surely turn into a full-on meltdown afterward, Jonah preps me by saying we can get burritos after I do it. This motivates me only slightly more, and I sniff in agreement, pissed that I even agreed to do this stupid thing.

Doug asks me to purchase a jar of honey. I go to the store and almost break down crying as I take it off the shelf. I imagine that there might be some residue still on the side or lid of the jar, and I squeeze hand sanitizer into my hand, as the woman shopping next to me with her teenager eyes me like I'm Cuckoo for Cocoa Puffs. I smile and squirt more of the stuff onto my red, destroyed hands. I look like a nut.

At home, I clear everyone out of the living room, and I set the honey on the table, placing a spoon to the side and a plate underneath. I hate that I'm doing this, and it feels completely unethical, like I am risking the safety of my baby.

Opening the jar, I can smell the wildflowers. The honey I chose is nothing extraordinary, but the scent and the amber color of the honey bring me back to summers at home in Boulder. I take the spoon and swirl it in the stickiness, imagining the thousands of tiny potential botulism toxins sticking to the sides of the glass. There was a time when I couldn't even use a glass jar, much less touch a jar containing honey. Now here I was, playing with fire.

§

My parents kept bees when I was in high school, raising two hives in our backyard. I became accustomed to the buzz of the little workers cohabitating with us. My parents became obsessed with beekeeping, my mama dressing in her white suit, going out to check the hives and the queen. She worshipped the queen, delighting us with beekeeper facts when we ate dinner at night, feasting on food straight from her garden – tomatoes, arugula, multicolored carrots.

The honey that our bees produced was out of this world. It had an umami taste, a taste that stayed on my tongue for the whole day, sweet and almost smoky. In the mornings, I would spoon it onto toast with butter, and when I was sick, it was medicine. When my parents scraped the trays into the stainless steel tub, the honeycomb would slide down, the perfect hexagonal patterns maintaining their shape. It was mesmerizing, and my mom would give me a piece of honeycomb to eat.

I take the spoon and try a tiny bit. It's delicious, and I feel sad. Honey was just another one of those things that was so sacred and important for me, then became tainted with my diagnosis.

What was medicinal became evil in my irrational state, a fear so strong I could barely be in the same room with it. I've become so avoidant, so trepidatious about living.

I close the jar, and throw it away in the kitchen. I did it, I did the exposure, and no one got hurt – but that was enough for today.

Chapter Twelve: **Taking the Edge Off**

Summer is ending in Alaska. It's rainier, and the wind whips down our block, making Matias trip when he runs on the pavement toward his friend's house. The sun appears a few days at a time, tempting us, flirting with us, until it seems to say, *Fuck no*, again and disappears for a week. Jonah and I walk in tandem, him pushing our toddler's green dino car, me carrying Romi on my chest, strapped in and cozy with an oversized beanie. I can feel his breathing through the fabric of the baby carrier, shallow but there. He's asleep.

I've taken to calling him Romi. I have a hard time with the grandiosity of the name we gave him, and I am struggling to admit that I might want to legally change his name to Romi Lev – Joyous Heart, in Hebrew. It feels more significant, more on the nose with who he is and who we are. Rome is a city, a feeling of power, but Romi literally means "joy," or "God's exaltation." Lev was the middle name we thought about using before one of my friends mentioned that she was also using it. I took it off the list in the moment, never considering for a moment that it was okay to have the same middle name as someone else.

§

Under the gray sky, Romi is nestled in his carrier, eyelashes wet with a few drops of rain. I stroke his chubby little cheek. He hums and spits bubbles while looking up at me. His eyes are so wild – olive green, with hints of gold in the rare moments that the sun hits the island. They seem to change as well, depending on what color onesie he has on. They even sometimes look like opaque jadeite, which I love. It's my favorite color. His eyebrows are so expressive, and his little hands grip my shirt every time I go to put him down.

It's an idyllic image, a young family walking together, enjoying the fall weather, but all I can see is imminent death. I look at Matias and just feel sad. He won't ever be this small again – we're all just getting older and older until we die. He's so cute that I cry more, imagining dying and not being able to remember his face, or hold him close, or even say his name. Then I look at Jonah. He could die at any point, on the boat during a job or even just from some stupid mistake at the unit one day. I can hear Matias saying, *I luh you, Dada*, at Jonah's funeral, confused and panicked. Then I look at Rome. He's so young he doesn't even have a personality yet or really any defining characteristics. But one day he'll be a person too, and I might get cancer and not be able to see him grow up.

What if there is an afterlife and it's like double-sided glass, where I can look at them but they can't see me? I guess that would be better than total oblivion. What if we die and then, in a poof, Cinderella-style, everything we've thought, felt, and known is obliterated?

I know I need to be on medication to help this.

Just take the damn drugs.

No, don't take medication. It's giving up.

I've heard both these statements more times than I can count over the past several years. I fought hard against it with Matias as a newborn. I can't expose my baby to potentially harmful drugs. What if it comes out that Zoloft causes cancer, or autism, or macular degeneration? I'll want to kill myself if I take it to chill myself out and then studies come out years later and it'll look like I was a selfish cunt who took the meds rather than keeping her baby safe. *Selfish bitch, I'm a selfish bitch.* If I end up exposing him to the SSRIs, I think I'll be like those moms in the '70s who took that anti-nausea drug and their babies were born with bizarre birth defects, limbs askew or missing.

Essentially, I feel like I'm not strong enough to keep my baby safe. If I take the drug, I'm putting my own well-being in front of my baby. And then I'd never forgive myself. And then life wouldn't be worth living, and then I'd be miserable until I died.

In this era of RFK and trad wives and all that, I feel even more inadequate. Women have been dealing with postpartum depression for an eternity. My own great-grandmother ended up in a psych ward for postpartum. She was never the same, or so I'm told. Thinking of a psychiatric hospital during the late 1930s in Vermont makes me feel queasy. I'm sure the women there were subjected to some weird experimental research that they will end up studying one day.

The Depression Kitty from *Big Mouth* sits on my chest every day at this point, and she only gets worse when Jonah and I argue. She curls herself in a ball and purrs while I settle deeper into the couch, only able to gather enough motivation to turn on the TV to numb out my brain to the drone of the candidates on *Love Is Blind*. Other than that, I go through the motions – changing diapers, making pasta, nursing and burping Romi, and reading to Matias. I look forward to each morning when I can stumble downstairs and drink iced coffee until I feel even the tiniest bit of energy.

I hit slumps during the day when I start thinking about death, and the intrusive thoughts consume me. That's when I zone out and start crying randomly. Matias is old enough at this point to realize that when I cry, it means I'm sad, and he runs over and grasps me with his little ravioli hands. I feel bad. This is bad parenting that he'll talk about one day in therapy.

I had to parent my mother, he'll say wistfully. *She had severe mental health issues.*

I hate thinking about that.

§

Doug calls me, and I feign interest in the conversation, pretending to be all right.

"Nola, I think it's time."

I know he means it's time to start meds. We've discussed it so many times, and he has recommended it to me over and over.

So I get the prescription that I set on the shelf in the hall closet, in the bag, lest any toxins from the medicine get on my hands and poison my family. Twenty-five milligrams of generic Zoloft, waiting for me. Before kids and during my anorexia era,

I would've popped one of those suckers no problem. Xanax was like candy, and my friend and I used to sit in my West Hollywood apartment on Beachwood and play Russian roulette with pills, opening up her backpack with the drugs her massage clients gave her and reaching in to take one. I'm sure I've tried Molly and Ecstasy, but I have no way of being sure. I had no responsibilities then and, honestly, not much to live for. I was singlehandedly keeping the Xanax business alive.

I call him back, Romi on my chest in the matcha-hued armadillo carrier. He's awake and lifts his little turtle head to look at me, greenish eyes big and inquisitive. I feel once again this sense of guilt, about taking a medication that will definitely pass through my breast milk, even if it's just a tiny bit. It doesn't matter how much. It makes me feel like a horrible mother.

Here we go, Rome. Let's start your lifelong dependency on SSRIs. It's only antidepressant medication that I'm hooking you on at a few months old. No biggie, dude. The withdrawal will be tough, but so are you, buddy.

I scoff at myself and place a paper towel on the counter, carefully taking one mint green pill out of the container. It's smaller than I thought – innocent-looking and oval. I grab a steak knife and saw along the centerline of the pill. It's called sertraline generically, which sounds scarier than Zoloft. Zoloft sounds like a Pixar character, not the name of a drug.

It's not quite clear why taking this is any different or worse than any of the other things I've done in my life. For some reason, though, I feel like I just agreed to streak naked through the set of *Good Morning America*. I'm shaking and my teeth are chattering from the nervous anticipation, and Doug smiles warmly over FaceTime. He's used to this. He's here for moral support.

I sheepishly hold up the quarter pill of Zoloft.

Ok, I'm doing it now. I throw it down the hatch and wash it down with some water. He claps and gives me a thumbs-up. I feel like Shamu, and I take a bow.

"Great job, Nola! This is the first step to making sure you show up for your family, and for your marriage."

I frown.

I don't want to have to take pills to make my marriage work. That doesn't seem fair. I already had to carry the babies in my womb for eighteen months, goddamn it.

Doug notices I'm a little pissed and tells me not to worry, that it will all be up from here. I'm not so sure, but he spends the next ten minutes trying to convince me. I zone out and pick at the cradle cap on Romi's head. It really bothers me, and I know I'll have to order a special brush to remove it so it doesn't keep spreading.

§

That night I start to feel something. It almost feels like I'm floating, untethered, but there is a distinct ringing in my ears. I try to make spaghetti and ignore the incessant pounding, almost drowning out the background noise of Matias and Romi needing to eat or needing to poop. I drizzle olive oil into the pan, watching it bead and disperse in the stainless steel. Adding pepper and garlic, I turn the heat too high, and I watch the black pepper almost coagulate and smoke. The dish is ruined, and I push it around for a few minutes before dumping the whole disaster in the sink.

I try again, feeling sleepier. The sun won't go down for another four hours, and I'm ready for bed. It feels like I drank a cup of coffee and my heart is beating fast, while simultaneously I could fall asleep sitting up. I change the boys' diapers and feed them almost in slow motion, completely checked out. Jonah keeps looking at me with concern, especially since I haven't laughed or gotten angry all day. I don't care what we watch on TV. I don't care if the laundry is done. I don't give a flying fuck whether the dishes are sitting in our disgusting sink. I am careless. Nothing matters; it's all good.

Nightmares torment me all night long, and I wake up dozens of times, sweaty and scared. In most of them I end up terminally ill or accidentally setting our house on fire. I wake up, and I'm alone in bed, the baby in his crib, which is pushed up against our mattress. I walk like a zombie to Matias's room, where I see Jonah, passed out like a corpse on his stomach on the carpet, his hand holding Matias's in his crib. He snores, and I put his arm next to his side. He's going to wake up with his hand asleep, and I know how much he hates that feeling.

I go downstairs and stare around the living room. The rugs are uneven, but who cares. I get myself a glass of water and stare at the four insanely bright area lights on the kitchen ceiling. When we moved here, I was shocked by the audacity of the builders to seemingly place all the light in the house in the kitchen. It is truly absurd. The rest of the house is dimly lit, but walk into the kitchen and you feel like you're about to be interrogated by the KGB. Doug went into hysterics when I mentioned this.

§

The pills make me feel worse. Over the next several days, any semblance of a personality that I had leaves. I feel like anorexic me is back, ready to boringly live out the rest of her life. I go from inconsolably sad to manically angry, slamming doors with any minor inconvenience. Everything is infuriating, but I don't have the energy to do anything about it. The tipping point comes when Jonah finds me in the fetal position after I tell him that I'm not in love with him, that this is doomed, and that I can't be with anyone. I'm sobbing, and he lowers himself to the floor, making the same shushing noise he does for Romi when he's losing his mind, too. I cry into my shirt, tits out, pushing my forehead into the gray laminate floor. He lies down and holds me like a little spoon.

"Shhh. Shhh."

"I can't do this," I wail.

"You don't have to, babe. If it's making you worse... you don't have to take anything if you don't want to."

He lays his piano hands on my face, where I'm unleashing all the pent-up hormonal and mentally ill energy I've been saving for months.

He is right. No one is forcing me to medicate. I tried it – I came, I saw, I didn't conquer. I'm not letting anyone down by not becoming dependent on an SSRI. I'm not even letting myself down. I don't feel anything like this; I feel nothingness. I'd rather feel things strongly, too strongly, than not at all. This feeling of emptiness takes away my will to forge on and *do* something. This is not how I want to live.

My husband picks me up off the floor and cradles me like our newborn baby. I close my eyes and hang on his neck.

Chapter Thirteen: **Black Cloud**

Three weeks in this time and I'm remembering the black clouds that enveloped me after a few weeks with Matias. I lay in bed every day, alternating between nursing, checking the CDC for updates on measles, and rotting on Instagram. The blinds are still shut and I just know the sunshine has hit its Sitka limit and we've had our fill of what we were given this year. The sun is done.

Rome is lying next to me on the evergreen linen sheets, sleeping soundly for the first time all night, although it's already well past 8 a.m. I know I should be hungry, and I should get up and go pee, but why? I don't need to get up. What's the point? There's nothing good to eat, and I can hold my pee in. The covers feel comforting, and I can finally just do nothing and let my varicose veins throb in peace. I got up once already to take my antibiotics, so there – I'm done moving for the day. Jonah can handle Matias. I'm kind of a bummer anyway and don't want to catch a glimpse in the mirror of whatever is happening on my face. I can imagine it's not appealing: drool and toothpaste in the corners of my mouth and goop in my eyes.

The rain is falling now.

Fuck my life I hate the goddamn rain.

I could go my entire life without ever seeing rain again and be totally fine. I pull my shirt up and check my boobs. Still red, still swollen, still leaking.

§

Two days prior, I had gone to bed feeling like someone was taking a hammer to my head. I was freezing cold, aching all over, and I felt a big lump forming in my left boob. I pushed and prodded the area, trying to make it go away with sheer willpower and a little bit of physical manipulation. Alas, no luck.

"Fuck, Jonah, I have another blocked duct!" I yelled out from the shower as I stepped in, careful not to trip over the potty chair placed precariously close to the tub.

"What?!" he yelled back while changing a diaper.

I suck in through my teeth. He's probably going to leave the trash on the floor again, diapers piling up next to the trash can. I hate that.

"I have to try to squeeze this out – please handle them both. I'm in fucking pain!"

The hot water feels great, except when it lands on my boobs, where it's like fire. I silently open my mouth, faking a scream. Postpartum is such a bitch. Jonah says he feels not great because he hasn't worked out. Everything he says makes me want to hit the wall. Hasn't worked out? I'd love my vagina to just work again. The current situation looks like a crime scene.

I massage my boobs, expressing milk all over the laminated shower curtain. Not helping. Each time I try to massage the lump, I start crying. I want my mom. But then she'd just say there's a reason men don't do this – women are the stronger sex. We are built to withstand more.

Nola, there's a reason why statistically women survive famine more. When I told Doug this, he mentioned the fact that it's true, men can't take as much – that's why the suicide rate is so high.

I go to bed and wake up with the worst headache of my life, confident now that this is the flu. The thermometer reads 99.5°F and my head starts spinning. *Oh no. I'm gonna give my three-week-old the flu. What's the survival rate of that? I can't do this; I can't do this.*

§

At urgent care I sit in the dingy office, waiting for the doctor. I look down and there's an enormous spider near my feet. Ice cold, I involuntarily shiver. *Are you freaking kidding me?* It's got to be the biggest spider I've ever seen. I text photos to about five people and get the feedback I don't want – it looks like a brown recluse. I stare at it, hoping to God it won't run over and bite me, but it is lazily making its way across the floor, swerving like a drunk driver.

The doctor comes into the room cheerfully after knocking. Wearing enormous acetate glasses the color of rubies, she asks me how I'm feeling and what my pain is. I say bad, but I can't focus because of the enormous spider on the floor. I get up and sit on the table. She knows I have OCD, and I tell her I'm scared the venom got on me when I sat on the chair where the spider may have walked. She smiles, the only reasonable and sane reaction to hearing someone say that.

"That's how my crazy brain works!" I laugh and try to move on to my boobs, an infinitely more interesting subject. She clicks through several screens on the computer while standing, and then redirects her attention back to me.

"Nola, are you feeling okay? You mentioned to the nurse you felt a little blue."

Lol. A little blue. I'm like the entire ocean at this point. I'm thinking a lot about existentialism and death. *What happens after this? I don't want to not think anymore! What happens to us when we die? I don't want to vanish. I don't want to never have the chance to hug my babies again. This is awful. Why does anyone do any of this if it all just goes away?*

"I'm doing okay," I lie.

She looks relieved and wipes her glasses with her sleeve.

"Well," she says, "if you do start to feel bad please let us know. We're here for you."

I feel horrible now, I think. *Help me, please.*

But all I say is thank you, make some quippy joke about how fucked up perinatal OCD is, and head out the door. She waves enthusiastically at me, trying to bring the sunshine back to my face. I fake a camera-worthy smile and leave, dousing my hands and lower arms in Purell before opening the door.

§

A month passes. I'm glued to my phone, doomscrolling Instagram during most of my free time, trying to drown out the uncomfortable thoughts. I tune out everything around me, and lie in bed after Romi nurses, going through the profiles of people I don't know and will never know. I don't know why I find these accounts so fascinating, but I just do. It gives me something to strive for. All I want is to buy everything I see on the internet, and I've calculated that I'll need probably $20,000 for all of it. Maybe if I slowly max out my PayPal account, Jonah won't notice, and I can feign disbelief when I finally come clean.

No, that's really bad. That would be motive enough for divorce. Poor Jonah.

I start noticing my vision is doubled, and I can't focus on anything close or far away. I try on my old glasses, but the same thing happens. *What the fuck.* This is not okay. I immediately go to the worst-case scenario and imagine going fully blind. I'm already monocular and don't have depth perception.

What the actual fuck, God! Are you going to add insult to injury? I lament to Jonah.

He tells me it's probably psychosomatic when I yell at him about it at the breakfast table over croissants and coffee.

"See?" I shout. "I can't fucking see the individual crumbs! Why don't you believe me?"

He sighs and wipes the buttery residue with a paper towel. I'm bothered by the little pieces falling like snowflakes on the floor. I stare at them, and he notices, leaning down and collecting the little pieces. It reminds me of the Coke bottle when Matias was born.

"Nola. I believe you. You just need to calm down. You look

absolutely hysterical right now."

I shoot him a glare and then walk over to Romi and lean down toward him, trying to discern whether or not what I see is what I normally would've seen before. I put my head in and out of the play pen, trying to see if changing angles will help. It doesn't, or at least I think it doesn't.

"It's probably screen use as well," Jonah adds. "You are on the phone all the damn time."

My heart sinks, and my feet feel cold. I gulp. That's probably it. I'm probably a selfish bitch who decided subconsciously to sacrifice her vision and her ability to see her babies for the momentary euphoria of using social media. What a loser I am.

Matias is on the ottoman, sucking his thumb and staring at me. I rush over to him and hold him in my arms, rocking him and consoling him.

"Mommy's okay, tutto okay amore..."

I try to make him and myself both feel better, but I can't help thinking I've made the biggest mistake of my life. Now I'm going to pay. And I'm so stupid. I have only one working eye anyway. Now I get to live in utter darkness. Fuck my life.

I look down at the hairs on his head, trying to individualize each one, shifting my gaze back and forth, trying to focus and unfocus, like a camera lens. Jonah continues drinking his latte, staring at me like I'm crazy. He throws his hands in the air.

"Jesus Christ, Nola."

I look at him again, glasses off, glasses on. He knows about cameras. He used to be a photographer in LA when we met. My eyes squint.

Wait... Jonah, hear me out. When you look at Matias from there, can you see his full face clearly or is only part of his face clear and then you have to shift attention to another part of his face? Or can you see the full thing together immediately?"

He just shakes his head sadly.

"Or maybe, is it that my brain can put together the picture because I know our son's face so well, but it's actually a figment of my imagination? Would that even be possible? Jonah, Jonah. It's like everything is buzzing, and I can't really get the full picture of what the boys' faces look like."

He just throws up his hands.

"I know I'm not crazy."

He smiles and goes into the kitchen to clean up. He's used to this by now.

I spend the rest of Saturday and Sunday trying to figure out if I'm seeing everything exactly as I was before. I convince myself that maybe I've been addicted to screens so long that I can't even remember, and I haven't seen clearly for years. Then I get very sad, lying in the bed with the blinds drawn for hours, trying to cry but unable to. I'm numb, numb, numb. I reckon with the idea of not being able to see anything ever again. I dramatically mention suicide because I'm, in my eyes, a horrible mother, selfish for using screens. I feel weak and bad for joking about suicide. I wouldn't actually kill myself, but I think about it often. Not about actually doing it, just like, *How would everyone feel if I was gone?*

§

I go to the eye doctor on Monday. There's only one in Sitka, and she lets me call her personal number. She's odd, overly familiar, and maybe lonely. She keeps mentioning wanting to get together for dinner.

"Sure," I say. "When I can see again, of course."

She checks my vision, leaning back triumphantly to tell me my sight changed again postpartum. I hold my breath, waiting for the bad part, but she surprises me.

"It's actually improved," she says, beaming. "Your old glasses were too strong. You need a 1.25 now."

I breathe out slowly. It must be a mistake. She lets me use the steampunk-looking practice glasses with the right lens, and I walk around the grungy office, making sure I can see. I come back in, asking why I can't see fully clearly no matter what.

"You've got something called accommodative spasm," she chuckles. It wasn't paranoia. "You're unable to focus because of the prescription, and because you're monocular, your eye gets more fatigued because of all the work being put on it all the time."

"What about screen time?"

She goes to the computer, looking in her database to see what else could cause this annoying grievance.

"So... looks like screen time, as well as some medications, like SSRIs."

FUCK.

My heart drops again. The fucking Zoloft I took for four days. I took it to be less depressed, and it's going to make me blind now. I literally could not be more depressed. It's almost ironic.

Four days, and I fucked myself. I'm such a piece of shit.

I sink down in the leather seat. She notices my change.

"But yes, it can go back to normal."

I'm barely listening, all I hear is "it can." *Can it NOT as well?*

"Looks like–" she continues reading off the monitor "–depending on severity, it can take several days to several weeks."

We can dream, I think.

§

Two weeks later, I go back to my OB-GYN for a checkup. Sitting on the tissue paper, I wait for her in the office. I've already got it in my head that I'm going to be telling her about my vision issues. I'm reminding myself of all the interesting points that I want to make about the changes in my vision, and mostly about my obsession with them, when she walks in. She looks at me and smiles sadly as she squirts Purell into her hands and sits down on the little rolly stool. I pull my sweater around my shoulders and stare back at her, smiling slightly and waiting for her to say something. I can already tell something is wrong.

"I'm so glad that you're doing so much better this time postpartum."

There's a pregnant pause. She runs her hands through her hair and leans forward on the stool.

"I do have to give you some news, though, and I'm so sorry that you have to find this out now. I never like doing this."

I shift on the paper, and it makes an obnoxious noise, like the cacophony of children opening birthday presents.

"What is it?" I say, now pinching my own thumb to try to prevent myself from tearing up if this is really bad. I pinch so hard my cuticle starts to bleed. She definitely notices.

"Well, you remember how we did a Pap smear on our last visit, right? I received the results from that a few days ago."

Oh God. She's gonna tell me I have HIV or HPV. I nod for her to continue.

"So, the results came back, and I'm really sorry to say that you have two strains of HPV."

I let out a huge sigh. She looks at her chart, as if looking for the right thing to say next. I clear my throat.

"Well, that – will that hurt the babies? Right now that's my main concern." I inhale audibly.

"No, they are totally fine. Like I said when we tested you, women with HPV have healthy vaginal deliveries all the time. What I need to tell you, though, is that the strains that you have are aggressive. They can lead to cervical cancer and need to be monitored probably every six months."

Fuck my life. I guess that's what I get for telling her that I probably had HPV while she inserted the speculum during our last visit.

I look at my doctor. She's typing whatever it is she needs to document into the computer. Some nurse knocks on the door, comes in, asks her a question, and walks back out. Her scrubs are an awful shade of teal.

Outside, it's raining. The sleet hits the windows and drizzles on the outside of the glass, resembling tears.

"Well," I quip, "I probably shouldn't have whored myself

around Southern Europe."

I laugh, and she doesn't. She smiles at me and then touches my knee.

"You're going to be okay, though, right? Do you feel all right about this?" She looks at me, asking me a question without actually saying anything. I don't know how to respond, so I resort to self-degradation – again.

"You mean, am I going to kill myself? No, I'm much too selfish for that. Plus, I'm a mother now. That would be so fucked up."

She pushes back her chair, obviously not amused, and asks me if there's anything else I need from her today. I space out on what I showed up for. I decided not to mention my vision. Who needs vision when you have a busted vagina and are now a newly HPV-laden leper?

I leave the office and walk to our car in the rain. I keep thinking of *Girls*, the show that pushed me through my teen years. *"All adventurous women do"* was the line that Lena Dunham's character typed into her Twitter feed.

What if I don't want to be an adventurous woman anymore, though?

I keep thinking about who could've given me the two strains. That makes me go through my mental roster of all the unfortunate sexual experiences I've had since I lost my virginity at sixteen. There were so many bad instances, and to be honest, I don't remember some of them. I can't believe I just let people do whatever they wanted and I didn't worry about germs or diseases or viruses. Maybe it was that my lack of self-respect was so much bigger than my fear of hurting myself. Whatever the reasons were, it doesn't feel worth it now.

I blink my eyes seven times for good luck and get in our car, ready to drive back to our house and into all my responsibilities. As I leave the parking lot, I blast ABBA on the speakers.

Chapter Fourteen: **Existentialism**

Most days I do okay, and then I think about death. As a kid I'd lie on my parents' bedroom floor, on my makeshift nest bed, thinking about what might happen after I die. I would look at the ceiling, perseverating on my imminent death. The corners of my mouth would turn down in a frown, and I'd want to scream into the navy darkness of the house. But I couldn't do it without my parents waking up, so I'd do what my dad said he'd done as a little kid – lie facedown on the pillow and push my eyes into the down feathers so hard I'd see stars. He said that took away the worry for a bit. It did.

Now I have an even more acute awareness of my mortality. As a new mom, I wasn't worried about myself at all, but when pregnant with Romi I started worrying about my own health and future too. If something happened to me during pregnancy, I'd be leaving Matias motherless, and if something happened to me after Rome was born, I'd be leaving two babies without their mama.

I look at them every day and feel profoundly sad. I hold Matias's head in my hands, brushing out his curls with my fingers, and I start crying. He is one and a half, doesn't know why I'm sad, but hugs my leg or grips my upper arms with his chubby toddler hands. I feel like a bad mother, with him comforting me. He has enormous, saucer-like brown eyes and blinks at me, muttering a mixture of Italian and English quietly in a high-pitched voice. He's perfect, and he'll never be this small, and all this goes away, and one day I'll be dead and I won't even be able to remember this. I'll just be nothing and everything will be gone. No consciousness, no memory, no ego or body. Dust, but even that is generous.

My eyes go blank as I think about all this while my toddler hugs me and my newborn cries in the crib next to us. I should go over and hold him. He'll never be this small again, and one day all my memories of him will be gone too. I will cease to exist, and after I die I'll never see them again. He's crying for milk, and I'm stuck in my chair. I don't feel anything at the moment, just meaninglessness – which in itself is a feeling, but one devoid of any sense of purpose. He keeps crying, wanting me or milk or something that I can't provide at the moment. I just can't get myself to stand up.

Every time I start thinking about what happens after death, my arms become a battlefield for my intrusive thoughts. At this point, they are ruined again, picked within an inch of their life. I used to do this as an anxious teenager, but here we are again, me at thirty years old, standing in front of the shower, picking until I bleed. It makes me look horrible and ugly, but I can't stop. The tiny level of satisfaction I get from getting a whitehead out is solace for my turbulent thoughts. It gives me a break from my broken brain. It's like a hiccup on the hamster wheel of shame and anxiety I ride all day. I go round and round in circles, trying to sift through the religious beliefs of different faiths, trying to find something that sticks. I desperately want there to be an afterlife where I'll reunite with my kids, husband, and family, but it's so hard for me to believe. Rationally, it doesn't make any sense. The Jewish belief focuses on making this life the best we can and not focusing so much on the after part, but that seems a little avoidant to me. How do you NOT focus on the after part? How do you get anything done knowing it'll all be gone one day? What's the fucking point?

Or maybe the Torah is right, and we will all go through a cosmic washing machine, rinsed clean of our wrongdoings and before ascending to wherever it is people go next. I don't care if it's heaven or hell. I just want to be able to be with my children again at the end of all this. It could be the DMV for all I care.

When you have a mental illness you spend every day wrestling with the desire to be open and honest about it or keep hiding it away. I remember jokingly saying I had OCD in sixth grade when I liked keeping my pens and pencils organized by color in my Japanese pencil case. Who did I offend then? I'm sure someone around me at school was suffering in silence. Now that I have it, it irks me when I hear people downplaying what I deal with daily. I pray every night. That might be the only aspect of my life the OCD monster hasn't swallowed up. And religious righteousness is a subtype of this disorder – people compulsively do everything they can to remain pious and not commit blasphemy or sin in general. Eek.

So I pray, because the only solace I've found through this entire hellish experience is faith. I'm not angry at God for giving me this illness or for making my left eye not develop in the womb. Everything happens for a reason. It's a lesson and there's a higher reason. I've been given so much good. Who would I be if I thought there wouldn't be any struggles or hurdles in my life?

§

Praying has always been a part of my life. Since I was little, I'd do it alone in my room before bed at night, quietly asking the God I believed in, though no one else at my house did, to make sure I woke the next morning able to see. I was so terrified of going blind that I found God. I was always aware that He existed, I just couldn't quite put my finger on what it was. I think I called it "magic" as a little kid, but then when I started becoming cognizant of my visual deficits, I finally got what I was looking for. I found it on my own, which in itself is a miracle and proof of the Divine.

My family's religious background is much like our ancestry: a mess of conflicting faiths and cultures. Not going back too far, my dad grew up in an upper-class Christian household, the son of immigrants from Canada. He remembers getting in trouble at church, probably because he has undiagnosed ADD, but that's beside the point.

I'm still not sure what my dad believes. I think he's probably agnostic, but his siblings are still Christian. My mother on the other hand, grew up with an Irish Catholic father from Queens and a mother who found Christianity at a young age, growing up in a household with no religion. We found this was because they were French/German Jews who came to America in the early twentieth century to give their family a fighting chance.

My Jewish family came from Alsace-Lorraine, France, though there is little documentation – partly because many Jews hid their identities for safety and because so many records were lost or destroyed. If you've ever seen *Inglorious Basterds,* it's the town where Tarantino filmed his movie. Alsace-Lorraine sits along the German border, a place that goes back and forth between France and Germany. It is home to a UNESCO World Heritage Site for French Jews and has one of the country's historically significant Jewish populations. It is known as the city that "anticipated" the Holocaust, and many families fled, immigrated, or created new identities for themselves and their descendants, including those who came to America at the turn of the century.

I named Matias after my great-great-grandfather, Matthias Wilhelm, who immigrated with his family to America at seventeen. They went through Ellis Island and ended up in Vermont. Occasionally I speak with my grandmother's cousin, who knows plenty about the family history.

"It's full of drama," she says in her Jersey accent. "Something about a priest, uh, I don't know, but something definitely went down!"

When I was pregnant with Matias, she sent me papers and documents she had collected over the years, a hodgepodge of records on the family and the curious circumstances that led them to New York on a ship a century ago. Jacques, my great-great-great-grandpa, had some falling out with a priest and, for some bizarre reason, left his successful farm, which his family had owned for generations, to go to America only to have nothing. His son, Matthias, was the sole breadwinner for years, working at a foundry. I have his obituary, where it's written that he loved opera and spoke over five languages fluently. He was a quiet man and didn't interact much. He was very cultured and very much someone who kept to himself. He died before my grandma was born, but she grew up with her German grandmother in the house.

I have always clung to my lineage, wishing that more in-depth accounts were taken of the people whose ancestral line I am carrying on. When I think of how depressed I am now, postpartum for the second time, I think that it stems from the fear of being forgotten.

All those people in my family line, including my son's fourth-great-grandpa, whom he was named for, all lived full lives. At the time, they probably felt immortal, like they would live to reach a ripe age, and then be remembered forever. They probably were talked about for a few generations after they died, but now, their memory wanes, and people have trouble remembering even something as simple as their name.

I don't want to be forgotten. I want to be remembered, and not just for where I lie in the family tree. It's frightening to think about the fact that I don't even know what color eyes my great-great-grandmother had, or whether or not she liked cream in her coffee. I wish I could meet those who are gone – it would make me feel better, understanding who and where I come from. I hope my great-great-grandchildren will hear stories about me and Jonah. I hope someone laughs and smiles, remembering my name, or a funny trait I possessed. I hope someone passes down my wedding ring to their daughter, explaining where it came from.

There is no way to be sure if religion has made my OCD better or worse. I watch YouTube videos of Chabad rabbis explaining the difficulty of struggling with a concept of an afterlife, and I read books about the Jewish perspective on life. I know I need to focus on living the fullest life I possibly can now, to not waste a day, to find joy in even the most mundane, but it's hard when I feel like I am on a ride that one day will stop.

§

I gravitated toward Judaism as a little girl, setting up my own menorah, and standing next to my friends as they practiced their Torah portions for their upcoming bat mitzvahs. I wanted to be a part of it, and on some subconscious level, I knew I had Jewish ancestry.

Upon discovering that, yes, I did have Ashkenazi blood on my mother's side, I jumped into learning as much as I could, meeting with rabbis to discuss the possibility of a Beit Din – a formal conversion, but for me, more like a "coming home" of sorts for those who have Jewish ancestry. I studied for months, joining the synagogue chorus and attending Shabbat services.

In the spring, I dipped into the mikvah, nestled between brownstones on the Upper West Side of Manhattan. I was accompanied by my rabbi, another rabbi, and our cantor. I cut my fingernails and toenails, brushed my hair, removed my clothing, and stepped into the pool. The blessings were said, the ritual performed in the pool of natural water, and I stepped out, newly handed the responsibility of reigniting the Jewish flame in my family that had burned out three generations back. At the bimah, I read from the Torah, repeated after my rabbi, and was given the Hebrew name, Laila – night. I carefully touched the pages without dripping water from the mikvah onto the scroll.

§

Every week, when I light the candles, Matias standing at my feet and Romi in Jonah's arms, I come down to earth. I don't feel untethered, I feel rooted in tradition. We don't always light them, and we never do it at the right time, but it doesn't matter. I feel okay about the fact that I will die one day – I feel like a part of the moving mechanism that is civilization. It feels okay to know that there is an expiration date to this. None of us know what comes after.

I close my eyes, saying the blessing over the candles, over the challah, over the Kiddush cup, and finally over our children. My husband and I make eye contact over the candlelight, finally breathing, arms tired from rocking them to sleep, feeding them, caring for them.

Matias sings, "Amen."

Chapter Fifteen: **Honey Chicken**

Two under two is a hoot. It's November, and at best, we get about three hours of sleep at night. We are moving through the weeks, just existing. So happy, but just existing in the moment to change diapers and wipe tears. I can't be bothered to cook much, so we eat a lot of butter toast and mac and cheese, plus tons of coffee.

There's a knock on the door. Jonah's boss is bringing over a hot meal for us as part of the military warmth-and-service-driven community we're now essentially a part of. I don't want to see anybody. The thought of having to even brush my hair makes me want to punch a hole in the wall, but it is sweet.

My mind wanders while I wait for Jonah to greet our visitors and let them know I am not feeling well and am about to go to sleep with the baby, who's been "very challenging." The excuse always works like a charm, since no one should argue with a tired mother, if they know what's good for them.

Matias is talking up a storm and running all over the place now. He can identify animals in both of his languages, listing the sounds each one of them makes. He looks exactly like his dad – Jonah's eyes, nose, lips, hair color, and smile. People stop us all the time on the rare occasion that we go out, telling us how cute our little girl is.

Thank you, yes, he is very cute. We feel very lucky.

I always feel awkward correcting someone, even though it's technically misgendering, and it's my child. I always feel like I should be apologizing to them instead, like I should have dressed him to make it more obvious that he is a boy.

I'm a mess, but I want one more baby. I feel like we're meant to have one more – a girl or a boy, who knows, but I feel like God or the universe is telling me it's part of the plan. Unfortunately, no one else thinks so.

"Oh, God, Nola." My mom is never subtle. "I don't think anyone could take you being pregnant again. Stop now and save us all please."

Another relative tells me that my body doesn't seem to do well when pregnant and doesn't seem to like it.

Gee, thanks. That makes me feel great... although I did manage to have two very healthy and fat babies, successfully. They back it up, by mentioning the veins.

Ah, the veins. Every time I look at the back of my legs I want to vomit – there it is, my distended vein right behind my left knee, almost looking like an extra finger. It's like someone put a thumb on my leg. It's so hideous, and I can't stand it, but like everyone tells me, it'll be there until I'm an old lady, so I better get used to it. I can't even shave properly because I'm scared I'm gonna hit it and bleed all over the bathtub, hemorrhaging out on our bathroom floor. The less I shave, the less I care about anything having to do with hygiene or personal care. I can't remember the last time I even wore ChapStick.

I think the veins are making me more depressed.

Depression is all-consuming. I look at everything wistfully, with melancholia. Even the drawers being put back into the dresser askew makes me sad. I don't know why, but I try to find the sadness in everything now.

Anything and everything can be depressing if you try hard enough – the lonely mushroom outside under the tree, the dishes stacked in the sink, my hair falling out postpartum in the bathtub, me using the drain weasel to scoop said hair out. Jonah tries to snap me out of it, either by being funny or scooping me into a hug. Neither works. The only thing that does is to buy stuff on the internet, but I ban myself from the credit card again because money burns a hole in my pocket. I know I can't be trusted not to shop my feelings away. It doesn't matter what it is. If it gives me that *ping* of excitement, I have to have it – it could be anything from a serving spoon to a pair of flip-flops, useless in Alaska.

In the mornings I sit, watching Jonah feed Matias Cheerios and banana in his highchair. The morning energy is nice, peaceful – but I can't do anything or talk about anything until I've had half a cup of coffee. It's the unspoken agreement in our marriage, and Jonah knows I'm unable to cope with anything serious or necessary before then.

This morning I've had approximately a quarter cup before the knock on the front door. I wonder what they have brought to us for a meal, I'm starving. I haven't eaten anything since the leftover pizza last night, and I need to eat to produce enough milk.

I hear Jonah thank his colleague at the door and then close it.

I hear him put something heavy on the floor. He walks back into the room, empty-handed. I look at him, confused. He rubs his hands together, obviously about to say something not ideal.

"So."

Uh-oh, this can't be good.

"So," he continues, "Brent and his wife just dropped off a bag of food. Really sweet of them. The thing is, babe..."

I motion for him to continue. Matias is chewing his cheerios like a cow chews cud – methodically, watching us and this interaction.

"I guess he didn't know we don't do chicken."

Gut punch. Chicken is in our house.

"Okay, we can just throw it out, and then I can clean the place where the bag was set down. It's okay, I've been working on this. No biggie. At least it's cooked."

I nod at him, showing him that it's all going to be okay. He scratches his head, tight-lipped, and I know that's not all.

"Except, that's the thing, it's not."

He grimaces, and my knees feel weak. Actual salmonella is in the house right now. I have been doing so well, managing my symptoms and compulsions when they arise by doing exercises that Doug has been teaching me. I'm utilizing all the techniques, but unfortunately, in every situation, salmonella wins.

"And," he says.

"And what?!" I am raising my voice at this point. He walks over to me and gets down next to me to break this next nugget of news.

"It's 'honey chicken,' Nola. The sauce is made of honey and spices."

I'm about to pass out. I lean back, slumping in my chair, out of breath. Raw chicken and honey together? Salmonella and botulism are the OCD lovechild I never knew I never needed. I'm picturing the raw chicken juice mixing with the sticky raw honey, permeating the airspace around our front door.

I immediately start planning. I'll have to use an entire bottle of vinegar, cleaning solution, and Dawn soap to clean the floor. Then I'll have to scrub the door handles that they touched. On top of all this, Jonah will have to shower because he touched the bag, and then I will have to shower after I clean. No matter if the rancid chicken was in a bag, the floor is still dirty.

Freak-outs like these usually take an hour to deal with, denting our weekend time with scrubbing rituals and do-overs when I feel like I haven't been thorough or have messed up in some way. I scrub until my hands are raw, or Jonah does it, taking my specific instructions.

The scary part of this is, during the summer, we had a tsunami scare. But to me, chicken and honey, especially mixed, are way more terrifying.

Tsunamis have nothing on food poisoning. Not even when we packed the entire car up, hearing the dull warning sound of potentially rising water.

"What is this?!" Jonah was so frustrated. "Are we, like, magnets for natural disasters?!"

He was nervous, and we both started laughing, scared. The last time we were hunkering down, scared of dying at the hand of Mother Nature, was when I was newly pregnant with Matias, in the bathtub at our Tulsa rental. Now here we were, in a different state, potentially escaping a tsunami, with me pregnant as a house with Romi.

We moved fast as we packed up the box of essentials – flashlights, diapers, peanut butter, wipes, warm clothes, water, crackers, and blankets. I turned the TV on to *Winnie the Pooh* in Italian for Matias and let him zone out, not wanting him to be stressed or freaked out by the commotion and chaos. My stomach was heavy at this point, legs swollen with varicosities, sweating even in the cold of the house. Jonah lifted everything while I checked off items on my mental list.

He toted jugs of alpine water to the back of the car, making sure we had enough hydration to last us for a few days, just in case. I stood at the front door, looking at the elevated steps of our townhome. I never realized it before, but the houses were elevated just in case the seawater rose. Smart.

Tsunamis have terrified me my entire life. The idea of a gigantic wave rising up and swallowing an entire city was definitely the subject of some of my nightmares, especially after watching *The Impossible*. We are on an island here, and though it spans fourteen miles of coastline, there is nowhere to go, except up in the mountains, and even then, the roads going to those mountains roads would be packed and inaccessible in the event of a tsunami. Everyone would have the same idea, and that means some people would still be stuck at sea level, to drown.

Jonah is levelheaded in an emergency. He moves calmly and carefully, doing what needs to be done, not running around like a chicken with its head cut off, like I wanted to do.

"We can't do anything about it," he reminded me. "We do

what we can. Beyond that, it's out of our control."

True, but hard to hear.

We got into the car and drove across the bridge and up to the high school, the so-called evacuation zone when tsunamis hit. As we sat in the car on the top of the hill, friends and family started texting and calling us, having heard about the tsunami warning for Sitka. There had been a massive earthquake off the coast of Russia, triggering a tsunami, and because of our proximity, the ripples–or whatever they are called scientifically–were causing smaller tsunami risks all the way down the coast. The baby kicked in my belly, moving his foot across the surface of my distended stomach, letting us know he was there. Watching his heel push outward, I panicked, thinking about what I would do if I went into labor in the car. *Would I freebirth outside in the rain in my compression socks?*

Parker McCollum played on the radio as we sat in the high school parking lot, and Jonah checked the weather and news forecast. We were still in the yellow zone, which told us to be aware, and there was definite risk. I nursed Matias in the front seat, lulling him to sleep with a Texan lullaby, and after several hours in the dark, we made our way sleepily back to our house, crawling into our bed, for once, without showering.

But chicken. Chicken is where the real danger lies.

Chapter Sixteen: **Shinrin-yoku**

It is Hanukkah, and our second holiday season in Sitka. Jonah will be leaving in five days to go to California, where he will train for a new job that will take us to a new state. We don't know where we'll go, but as long as it's not Alaska or somewhere like Guam, I'm game for anything. I just need to get in the sunlight.

My mom sends me reels and posts on social media about the importance of the sun, of the UV rays touching your face in the morning before ten a.m.

"Some people even swear it cured their PTSD," she says, exuberant.

"That sounds great," I say. "That is, if we had any sun up here." I decide not to mention the new fad sweeping social media: sunning one's taint.

Whenever my parents visit, they are shocked again by the lack of sunlight and the overkill rainfall that plagues the southern Alaskan rainforest. It's pretty miserable, and both of them start to get cabin fever whenever they stay for more than a week. Everything is wet, damp, and dark. It feels like when you watch a period war film, where the entire story takes place in darkness. We are used to it, but the folks that visit us aren't.

We show them around the island, all fourteen miles of it – the coffee shop, the one Mexican restaurant, the two grocery stores, and the most exciting thing: the new hospital that is being built. Everyone feigns excitement, when it feels like we've just toured them around a set for a middle school play.

"You'll never forget this experience," they say.

That's for sure. I definitely will never forget living in Alaska, a state I never even thought to visit. And now we are going to be leaving – I just have to survive two months on my own first, without Jonah. Easy peasy.

§

On the last night of the Festival of Lights, we cuddle on the couch. I cling to him like a barnacle. There are presents strewn all over the floor, low-stimulus toys for Matias, because, yes, we are *those* parents. We even returned a toddler coffee machine because it made too much noise and didn't give him enough freedom to use his imagination.

Matias loves Hanukkah, and like Pavlov's dogs, figured out that after we lit the candles and sang some songs, he would be opening a present. Like clockwork, after lighting the Shamash and the candles on the menorah, he would run to the Christmas tree, pick a present, and start to rip tiny bits of wrapping paper off. Jonah would slow him down enough for us to grab our phones to film him opening his gifts. I think we enjoyed it even more than he did. His eyes sparkled when he opened each new thing, smiling from ear to ear. Books are his favorites.

I stretch my legs out over Jonah's. My body is starting to resemble something I recognize again, without getting to that point of, "Oh, no – she's too skinny." You can finally see the shape of my jaw again, the definition in my arms, and the shape of my waist. I don't have three chins, which I got very comfortable with during pregnancy. I am no longer trying to contort my body into becoming heroin chic, and I feel at peace with how I now look. If my boobs stay like this, I'm content to breastfeed forever. They are glorious and seem like consolation prizes for having my body go through labor twice in two years. I have faint indentations on my hips, from where my skin expanded to make room for my growing tummy. The skin is soft, and Romi grabs at it like a comfort blanket when he's sleeping on my chest during a contact nap.

Jonah rubs my feet as I lean back and close my eyes.

"How am I going to pull this off?" I ask him, incredulous. I point my toes.

"You're going to be fine, honey. Your parents will both come and help you. And at the end of this, we'll be moving elsewhere and we can get off this island and try to start life again, not afraid of everything."

I sigh. That sounds very nice. I'm not going to miss it here. I've started calling the island Shitka instead of Sitka, and the patent is pending.

"Also," he notes, "I'll have my phone – this isn't like boot camp. We will all be totally fine."

He gives me a kiss and I hold his head in my hands. I love this man. No one has seen me more at my best, and more at my worst, and vice versa. We never gave up on each other, on our love.

"Do you think a lot of people struggle early on in their marriage?" I ask him.

He closes his eyes, head laid on my shoulder. His hair smells like coconut.

"I think so," he replies, "although I don't think people talk about it. I think everyone wants to appear like they have it all together, when in reality, most of us don't."

I feel scared that people are judging us because our struggle was so public and obvious. It makes me feel really insecure. I turn my head to place my nose in his hair, inhaling his scent, which always, since that winter four years ago, has felt like home. He holds my hand and squeezes it with both of his. We don't say anything else, but listen to music.

§

"All Yourn" by Tyler Childers is playing, and while the snow starts to fall outside in the dark Sitka night, Jonah pulls me up off the couch to dance. We haven't done this in forever, and it's something we always loved to do while dating. Whether it was a Nashville dance hall or a wedding in Houston, we always found each other in the rhythm – synchronized, in tandem. Dancing together, the rest of the world was always drowned out, a place where we didn't pay attention or care about the opinions of others.

I place my head on his chest and start crying a little bit.

The past two years have stretched me further than I ever thought possible, inviting me to dive into the deepest parts of myself, of my wounds, and of my marriage. The beginning of our marriage was a trial by fire – baby, boot camp, separation, mental illness, dislocation, another baby, and now isolation.

We dance like we did at our wedding, clinging to each other, with the storm cracking and pouring down around us. During our first dance, the power went out. What went from the hottest day of the year turned into the biggest summer storm, and thirty seconds into the dance, it all powered down. We hugged, the torrential downpour around us, and Jonah leaned down to make sure I was okay.

That day was beyond taxing, but the one moment I felt okay was when it was just us two, alone. So standing on an East Texas porch in a June downpour felt like I wanted to feel, tuning out all the noise, all the crazy, all the interfamilial chaos around us. I was pregnant with Matias and didn't know it, and everything about our wedding day seemed to be disjointed, disorganized, not what we envisioned. The rain was so apropos, seeing as it represents fertility in many cultures.

But on that porch, as the lightning cracked overhead, everyone started singing John Legend's "All of Me," off-key, with their phones in the air, and we swayed. The singing was so bad, but the sentiment was so sweet.

"Are you okay, my love?" Jonah leaned into my ear and asked me, holding the small of my back.

I held him closer. I really had not been okay up until that point, and he had sensed it. I felt like the wedding had run away from me, like a horse out of the gate. I had lost the reins somewhere at the beginning of the week.

"I am now," I said.

He kissed me, and my heartbeat slowed to a normal pace.

We learned to tune everyone out.

When the song finishes, we sneak upstairs, with Romi asleep in Jonah's arms, to watch Matias sleep. He's tucked into his bed, sucking his thumb serenely in his sleep.

"We made some really cute babies," I say, sidling up to Jonah.

He beams at me. Romi is sleeping with his mouth open, looking like Yertle the Turtle. Matias resembles the Lorax more. We lay our youngest in his crib, making sure he is in a safe position. Before I do, I kiss him on his steamed bun cheeks. He really does smell like soy sauce, and I breathe it in, wanting to bottle it up so I can always remember. Scent is so evocative and makes me nostalgic. My grandma always wore Opium by Yves Saint Laurent, and I can't walk into a Sephora without beelining to the perfume section in search of a bottle. Soy sauce is much easier to come by.

§

The first week that Jonah is in California, I am so busy that I don't have time for OCD. My parents are coming in ten days to help me, and I count down each day, celebrating each day as a victory. I go through the motions of mothering, waking up at six a.m. to change diapers, nurse Romi, and get Matias downstairs for breakfast. I self-medicate with caffeine to keep myself going, splitting up my coffee intake twice a day, so I never have a lull in my energy.

Matias is easygoing and can sit for an hour reading to himself while I handle the kitchen and his younger brother. He snacks on bananas, power bars and yogurt, and I sit and feed Romi, who is now, as my dad says, "waking up." It's almost as if he's figured out who each of us is and stares at our faces with the most skeptical look I have ever seen on a child. He furrows his brow and sticks his tongue out, and I've started calling him our little mob boss. He even has the tiniest underbite.

The only time fear really creeps in is when I have to go outside with the boys. I worry I'll forget one of them inside and lock myself out, or that I'll accidentally drop Romi, or that a dog will attack us on our walks. I don't venture far from home, but it seems like walking on the moon in comparison to the amount of agoraphobia that plagued me for the past year and a half. I slowly become more comfortable with the smell of cigarettes and diesel and have stopped showering every time we come back inside. It's just too exhausting.

The trash is also a struggle. I am very afraid of fecal matter still, and whenever I have to take the trash out, I have to load all the poop into the back of the car. It smells like fresh hell, and I put my head out my window, trying not to breathe in the shart particles wafting up from the back of the car. I look like a Labrador, but it's effective.

Since we can't use our personal trash cans due to the bear problem, all of our waste stays in the dry room until we drive it, or walk it, to the communal trash cans. I have a hard time finagling a good way to solve the problem of managing two kids while disposing of human feces. I make it into a riddle, forcing myself to strategize, elaborate with a step-by-step plan of how I get one kid in the car, then the other, then the trash, and then do it all in reverse when I've lifted the lid of the communal trash can ever so delicately. I saw our neighbor disposing of a bear carcass that he and his wife shot the other week, and I wanted to barf. They told me they were going to cook some meat in the backyard, and did I want to try some, and I declined, as politely as I could.

"Aren't you worried about trichinosis?" I asked him, incredulous.

"Nah," he said, "You just have to cook it at a high enough temperature."

I shook my head. No meat is good enough to risk worms.

§

Between my parents' visits, I take the boys on strolls along the little path behind our housing complex. I see the way Matias looks at the trees with wonder when we walk, and I know I am doing something good for him. We wander through the woods, and I start to panic about the bear that was spotted in the neighborhood a month ago, but my rational brain tells me that it's nothing to worry about now. I bite my lip until it bleeds, picturing myself running with my two children strapped to me with a bear lumbering close behind.

We don't talk as we walk, but I watch my babies' breath in

the cold air, and sometimes I whistle, Matias clapping for more, more, as we continue our walk around Japonski, the little island in front of Sitka, where our townhouse is. The road is icy at this point, but as we move through the forest, down to the water at the bay, I look up and stop. The trees create a canopy above us, inside the Pacific rainforest. I remember reading a book about the Japanese concept of forest bathing. The Japanese believe that when one walks through the trees, one partakes in immersion of the senses, receiving a metaphorical and symbolic "bath" from the trees. It's called *shinrin-yoku* and was developed in the eighties. A friend in Los Angeles told me that it decreases cortisol level and helps immunity and anxiety, but I never actually tried it, so now I do.

I ask my toddler what he can hear, see, smell, touch, and feel, engaging all the senses. I know he can't respond to all of these questions, but I can, and so I explain to him what is happening around us, from hearing the crows sitting on branches, to smelling the fresh, wet pine. He's quiet, but his eyes open wider, drinking it all in. I tell him what each color looks like, comparing the leaves to emeralds, the clouds to pearls, the icy water to sapphires.

§

That evening, after a dinner of fried eggs on toast, Jonah calls us from base. He's excited, and waits for me to sit down before telling me what's going on. I'm in my pajamas, with vomit all over my shirt from Romi, who used me as a personal mop earlier that afternoon. The phone connection drops for a minute, and I call him back. He asks me if I'm sitting, and I sit down to tandem nurse both boys, which makes me feel like a glorified heifer. Moo.

Jonah pauses before continuing, building up the anticipation. He's most likely on his fifth coffee of the day.

"We got it, babe!"

His face lights up, and he looks healthy. I haven't seen him look like this in two years, slight tan on his skin, using his teeth to smile. His hair is lighter too, and his blue eyes are brilliant, aquamarine and vibrant. I didn't think we were supposed to find out our location this early. I thought there would be more time, and I'm taken by complete surprise. I turn the volume down on the phone, I don't want to hurt Romi's ears.

"Did you find out where we're going to be moving? Oh my God, did you?" I spit out, while mentally preparing myself to hear that we'll be going to Detroit or something. That would be almost as bad as Alaska.

"California, Nola, we're going to California!" he yells into the phone, and I jump up. I can't believe it. I cannot believe it. All the dark days, all the time spent in the house watching the rain come down hour after hour, all the times I wanted nothing more than a Frappuccino and couldn't go get one – they were all coming to an end. There was suddenly a finish line in sight. Maybe God was truly smiling down on us.

§

We still had a month and a half before we would get to leave this godforsaken place, but we were on our way. The idea of California made me feel like I had found El Dorado, the Promised Land, the Goose with the Golden Egg. It felt like the forces that be had given us a chance to be happy again, to be living under the sun again, like humans are supposed to do.

Jonah had once been driving the boat with some colleagues, who were gushing over how much they loved living in Alaska. Jonah sat there quietly, and when they asked him how much he loved Alaska living, he chuckled. They couldn't believe that he didn't love to fish or hunt.

"I'm a real man," he said. "I buy my food in the grocery store."

Everyone laughed, even though he was only half joking.

Neither of us felt like we fit in, and we both realized that we missed the West Coast, the way we felt in a city as big as Los Angeles. We had met there. It was the beginning of our story, and now, here we were, full circle, heading back to the place where it all started. Six months earlier, it would have felt like the scariest prospect ever, moving to a town with more than the eight thousand here in Sitka, but now it felt like a dream come true, like a chance to start again and reclaim who we were individually, but also who we were together, as a family.

Chapter Seventeen: **Ion Bath**

The eucalyptus trees line the roads here, protecting cars through the winding roads down to Dillon Beach. I feel nauseous, Matias has already vomited up the Greek food from today's lunch all over a sweater in the back. I turn my body around and see both boys in the mirror. Romi is cooing, smiling while trying to push up on his car seat to see his older brother next to him. Matias is singing "Do-Re-Mi" as he watches the cows fly by the window. There are tons of them – they are beautiful, with soulful, sad eyes. I recognize the names of organic butter and milk brands as we drive past. *Oh, so that's where my food comes from,* I think. Both boys are dressed in colorful sweaters, the dappled sunlight from the car window illuminating every fuzzy strand of wool. I watch Romi's little hands grasp at dust particles in the air as Matias claps his hands while doing his best to imitate Julie Andrews. I'm impressed – he's two.

Jonah is driving, sipping his iced coffee while we listen to Noah Kahan on low. It's depressing and comforting music. I shield my eyes. The sun is so bright here. Or maybe it's not. I just haven't been under the sun in two years, and I guess I just don't remember. It's bright, though. It hits my arms and legs through the car, and I think about the whole sunning-your-taint thing on the internet. Seems legitimate. Like eating raw steak and bull testicles. Yum.

Two days earlier, we'd stopped on our twilight walk to watch two cows munching grass at the property line. One was completely black; the other had a white spot covering half her face. Crickets chirped, and Matias held Jonah's hand as Romi kicked in the carrier on my chest, his little head smelling like a corn chip.

The cows looked up at us while chewing, with those same sad, deep eyes. I was mesmerized, watching them watch us. The one with the spot meandered over to her friend and started licking her face, grooming her slowly, her thick eyelashes brushing the wet nose of her companion. The other cow just stood there, patient, making eye contact, at peace.

I started crying.

It felt so animal and yet so human – every being on earth is just trying its best, isn't it? I wanted to communicate to the cows that I saw them, that this moment was real and important to me. Before all this, I never would have noticed or cared about something as small as what had happened in that moment.

I stayed and watched them as Jonah walked up the hill with Matias. I didn't want to leave the cows.

I had become attached.

I had a burger last night, and now, watching these bovine beauties, I think I won't anymore. I feel guilty, but stop because I'm starting to feel carsick. The road continues winding as we make our way toward our destination, the ocean. I am exhausted – leaving Sitka felt like an evacuation, like a serious *Ocean's 8* operation with two babies. Never mind the fact that my dad helped me and I had packed approximately five pounds of hand sanitizer, it was a fucking nightmare. Four flights from our little Alaskan island to San Francisco, and we arrived disheveled and feeling something akin to violated. The upside was that Matias didn't poop, so I didn't have to use the public restroom for him. Baruch Hashem.

§

Every takeoff, every landing, I gripped my Magen David around my neck and used all my magical thinking skills to get the airplane to work. When I was ten, I remember thinking the fate of any given airplane was within my grasp. All I had to do was kiss my hand and then touch the door entering the plane, step in first with my right foot, and then smile and greet the flight attendants. In my defense, it felt like solid logic at the time.

The trip itself was just like one huge held breath. I was nervous my dad was going to have a meltdown while caring for his two grandsons, his palpable anxiety crowding mine. He was the one who surely passed that torch down. He managed to pass it down to both of his children, lucky us.

Somehow, we made it—four flights down to San Francisco—and upon arriving, I finally let out my breath. Thank God. I thought for sure I would've melted down during at least one of the flights, but I guess the old adage is true: moms always keep it together.

Calm in chaos, calm in chaos.

When the opportunity to leave Sitka came, we grabbed it. Even just the idea of the sun, wherever in the country or world we might be, was so appealing I cried. I missed the fucking sun. Dank, depressing, detrimental, devastating was how I categorized Alaskan living to the barista at the airport coffee shop. She made a face that said, *sheesh,* and busied herself making my double espresso latte. As she steamed the milk, I told her how I didn't even say farewell to the island, even when I was asked if I wanted to go say my goodbyes. *Fuck no!* I said, laughing, as I shook the turbinado sugar packet. She raised her eyebrows at me. *Unhinged mother.*

We landed at SFO on an overcast afternoon, and I am sure I looked like someone who had been surviving on a deserted island for years. Mussed hair, not washed recently, milk stains all over my sweatshirt, oil stains on my pants from healthy baby food packets, a baby in a front carrier and a toddler in a stroller, dragging bags behind me. *Get me to the Promised Land!,* was the only thing on my mind. I was like a horse to the barn. When Jonah saw us, he ran over, ready to take us to our new home. Matias leaped into his arms, little shoes dangling as Jonah squeezed him tight, tears in his eyes.

§

The road narrows, and Jonah purses his lips as he concentrates. I put my feet on the dashboard, gingerly rubbing my varicose-vein-laden calves, undisturbed by the lack of safety precautions I'm taking at the moment. My feet feel so good under the sun, but they are whiter than white. I look like panna cotta.

"We're almost there."

My husband turns around quickly to check on the babies. I twirl my hair up into a French twist with the clip in my mouth, placing it. I like the color. It's almost like jade, and it makes me uncharacteristically happy. "Orange Juice" plays on the car speakers. Then I notice it. There's poison hemlock along the side of the road. Oh dear God. I breathe shallowly, panting like a dog.

How do I do this again? Do I breathe in three seconds and then out? Or do I whip around and demand we go home?

I know I have a choice to make about how I respond to this. I close my eyes, willing the poison hemlock to disappear. Maybe if I wait ten seconds it'll be gone when I open my eyes, just a momentary imperfection in our fantastic drive through the Sonoma countryside. I peek out the window.

Actually, it's everywhere. Great.

"That's... hemlock, right? Jonah?"

I'm obviously hyperventilating, and he shifts his head in my direction, motioning that he is listening to me, all the while driving carefully.

Jonah is gripping the steering wheel, and I'm about to drive our good day off the side of the road. He knows the whole afternoon could blow up in an instant. It all depends on how far I'm going to take this. His knuckles are turning white and I can feel him bristle, scared I'm going to lose it and become hysterical. I reach out and I touch the nape of his neck, and he pauses, eventually relaxing into my hand.

"It's okay. I know it's okay, okay?"

He glances over at me, imploringly, as if asking me to please temper myself, still not sure if this is the calm before the storm. It's not that, but he doesn't quite trust it yet. It's not normal behavior from me, but it is better. I'm getting better.

"Yes, honey."

Jonah has turned full-caretaker mode. He smiles at me, and then chuckles.

"It's totally okay. The plants are not going to jump up and attack us. No risk of them ambushing our car."

I let out something akin to a laugh. Maybe this is us, again. Maybe we'll fall apart at the seams laughing while we binge-watch reality TV in bed together, sharing a pint of mint chip ice cream. Maybe we are arriving. Maybe this is what marriage and parenthood are supposed to feel like. Maybe mental illness isn't a sin, like someone had told me. Maybe I am becoming closer to who I used to be. Maybe becoming a mother didn't kill me completely.

"I love you."

He says it back, and I shift into my seat. Life is softer now, like the words we now share with each other. The sharpness is worn down from overuse, and our relationship is now tended to with care. It feels like we made a diamond of our marriage from the unmatched tension and strife. We created something beautiful, and now unbreakable.

I can now see the ocean, down the hill, past the bungalows. It's deep and blue, vast and inexpressibly wonderful. It's salt and minerals, and negative ions of aquamarine, cobalt, indigo, and emerald.

"Matias, look!"

I turn around in my seat to try to point out the endless ocean in front of us.

"Mommy, hold it. Mama, hold it!"

He holds his arms out, mimicking holding a gigantic beach ball. I hold his warm hand.

"We can't hold it, baby; it's too big – the ocean is THIS big! It's unholdable!"

My eyes widen and he smiles at me, food still all over his face from lunch. He's so cute, and I can't believe we made two of them.

§

Once parked, we surveyed the area. There are a few couples, dogs in tow, walking along the water's edge. Beyond that, almost no one is there on a Thursday afternoon. Wind swirls the sand into mini twisters around our feet, and I carry Romi as Jonah convinces Matias to go shoeless. I kick my leather flip-flops off to the side, careful to avoid the seagull poop near where our feet step. Jonah is already on top of it. He sweeps our eldest into his arms. The sun is hiding behind scattered clouds, reminiscent of a Georgia O'Keeffe painting, the one with the almost militant-looking cloud formations, stacked like bricks. I walk in front of Jonah – toward the ocean that I haven't seen in years. My feet feel so good in the sand – grounded, alive, finally.

At the water's edge, the waves lap up at my ankles, kissing my skin with cold. Romi is snuggled into my chest, nestled in my sweater like a little koala. I want to get in. I need to get in this water.

Jonah takes the baby from me, and I tactfully remove my clothes down to my simple bikini. I straighten my back and look at the goosebumps appearing everywhere on me, like an orange. I look at my varicose veins and my dry, scaly skin that hasn't seen daylight in three years, since I was in Destin, the day I found out I was pregnant. Same bathing suit, different ocean, different body, different woman.

I walk up to my thighs into the Pacific. There was a time when I would swim in this water every day, drying my body on the beach in Malibu, running along the sidewalks in Venice to meet friends to play volleyball and dance all night next to the water. That Nola doesn't exist anymore. She made that choice of putting the maiden to rest and becoming a mother. I met Jonah two blocks from this ocean, years ago, when obsessive-compulsive disorder still seemed like a funny quirk that some people struggled with. Now here I am with the family that I helped make, the boys who will also grow up loving the ocean.

It's so cold, but I feel warmth through my body. I'm smiling – something that I haven't done much of recently. The water sways, and I sway with her. Sunshine is peeking from those clouds and I feel something familiar, yet new. Hope, perhaps. I'm finally ready to shed this chapter, this unraveling, this spiral into the dark and unknown. I keep dreaming of shedding this skin, like a rattlesnake, and letting go of the encasement of fear I've been surviving in, small, compact, and hidden.

I'm craving light. Lightness of mind, lightness of spirit,

lightness, lightness, light. I don't need to be Atlas anymore. I don't need to hold up the whole world, protecting everything and everyone from every possible risk. My job is to live in this world and love. And maybe even eat some chicken.

My fingers skim the surface of the water, and I pull my hair back into a bun. It's time.

I jump in – I'm alive.

Acknowledgments

To Marni, thank you for holding my hand during pregnancy all the way from the other side of the world. Your friendship means everything to me, and I don't think I could've done it this second time without our endless voice notes and facetime calls. You're the strongest woman I know.

To Chloe, you are the big sister I never had. Thank you for your honesty, your loyalty, and your sisterhood. When I need someone to be real with me, I'll always call you.

To Jens, thank you for living the OCD fever dream alongside me. I've been so lucky to call you a bosom friend for my entire life, you helped me find the "funny" in the tragic. You're a mensch.

To Peter, thank you for being a constant since we were children. No one has known me the way you have through every period of my life.

To my editor, Mike, thank you for being the first to read these pages. Your support and expertise made this memoir come to life.

To Barış, thank you for bringing this book to completion with your art and design. You've so beautifully captured this story, and I am so grateful.

To Lena Dunham, your courage to lay it all out there gave me the balls to do the same. You're a queen. I hope we get to have a coffee together one day.

To Margo, I love you. I feel so lucky to be your sister, and I don't even have to write all of this. You just know.

To H., you taught me to trust myself again. Thank you for letting me lean on you for years. You're one in a million.

To the grandparents of my children, I love you. Thank you for being such a strong support system.

To my parents and my grandmother, I love you three. Thank you for putting up with my rage, my despair, and my crazy.

To my mother, thank you for truly making this book happen. You have always believed in me, (maybe too much sometimes!), and now as a mother I understand you so much more.

To Jonah, thank you for encouraging me to write this book, and being open to sharing the most intimate details of our life. I am so proud of how far we've come, and I'll love you till the day I die. You're my forever.

To Matias and Romi, I love you, sweet babies. You are my favorite part of being human. Thank you for making me a mama.

About the Author

A Coloradan at heart, Nola Samuels obtained her bachelor's degree in Chinese from the Università Ca' Foscari in Venice, Italy. After graduating, she moved to Manhattan and studied Musical Theatre at the American Musical and Dramatic Academy. Nola has worked in the fine art world, as well as a middle school ESL teacher. She lives in California with her husband and two boys, and in her free time she paints, reads, and obsesses over everything. Nola is an advocate for maternal mental health awareness and hopes her writing will help other women reach out to get the help they need and deserve. This is her first book.

www.ingramcontent.com/pod-product-compliance
Lightning Source LLC
LaVergne TN
LVHW100729061126
851857LV00011B/459
9798234109224